COCKTAILS 2013

FOOD&**WINE**

FOOD & WINE COCKTAILS 2013

EXECUTIVE EDITOR **Kate Krader**
DEPUTY EDITOR **Jim Meehan**
EDITOR **Susan Choung**
ASSISTANT EDITOR / TESTER **John deBary**
COPY EDITOR **Lisa Leventer**
RESEARCHER **Michelle Loayza**
EDITORIAL ASSISTANT **Danielle St. Pierre**

DESIGNER **Michelle Leong**
PRODUCTION MANAGER **Matt Carson**
FOOD RECIPE TESTER **Justin Chapple**
RECIPE ASSISTANT **Gina Mungiovi**

PHOTOGRAPHER **Lucas Allen**
FOOD STYLIST **Simon Andrews**
STYLIST **Suzie Myers**

ON THE COVER **Pab's Buck, page 82**

AMERICAN EXPRESS PUBLISHING CORPORATION

PRESIDENT / CHIEF EXECUTIVE OFFICER **Ed Kelly**
CHIEF MARKETING OFFICER / PRESIDENT, DIGITAL MEDIA **Mark V. Stanich**
SVP / CHIEF FINANCIAL OFFICER **Paul B. Francis**
VPs / GENERAL MANAGERS **Frank Bland, Keith Strohmeier**

VP, BOOKS & PRODUCTS / PUBLISHER **Marshall Corey**
DIRECTOR, BOOK PROGRAMS **Bruce Spanier**
SENIOR MARKETING MANAGER, BRANDED BOOKS **Eric Lucie**
ASSOCIATE MARKETING MANAGER **Stacy Mallis**
DIRECTOR OF FULFILLMENT & PREMIUM VALUE **Philip Black**
MANAGER OF CUSTOMER EXPERIENCE & PRODUCT DEVELOPMENT **Betsy Wilson**
DIRECTOR OF FINANCE **Thomas Noonan**
ASSOCIATE BUSINESS MANAGER **Uma Mahabir**
OPERATIONS DIRECTOR (PREPRESS) **Rosalie Abatemarco Samat**
OPERATIONS DIRECTOR (MANUFACTURING) **Anthony White**
SENIOR MANAGER, CONTRACTS & RIGHTS **Jeniqua Moore**

ISBN 978-1-932624-55-7
ISSN 1554-4354

Published by American Express Publishing Corporation
1120 Avenue of the Americas, New York, New York 10036

Manufactured in the United States of America

The names of companies and products mentioned in this book are the trademarks of their respective owners. Reference to such third-party companies and/or products is for informational purposes only and is not intended to indicate or imply any affiliation, association, sponsorship or endorsement.

F&W COCKTAILS 2013

FOOD&**WINE**
BOOKS

American Express Publishing Corporation, New York

PALOMA ITALIANA **P.76**

CONTENTS

TAWNY LITTLE BLOOD **P.156**

FOREWORD

When the F&W Cocktails series launched in 2005, people talked about just one style of gin—London dry—and stores carried only about a dozen labels. Accordingly, our recipes called, simply, for gin. Today there are hundreds of incredible gins in several styles—Old Tom, Plymouth, New Western, genever—and the recipes here reflect that availability. You'll find similar variety in other spirits featured in our book, from rum to tequila to liqueurs.

This transformation is part of the cocktail revolution that's bringing creative drinks to all corners of America. Denver now has four entries on our list of the country's 100 best new bars, including Williams & Graham, a 1920s-style speakeasy hidden behind a door disguised as a bookcase. Minneapolis has two entries; Eat Street Social's Ira Koplowitz and Nicholas Kosevich contributed the Suze Bramble (**P.32**), a riff on the classic gin-and-blackberry Bramble, made with blanco tequila. We also document fantastic bar food like the crispy Manchego cheese fritters (**P.179**) from Portland, Maine's Carmen at the Danforth; the recipe is one of our favorites.

This book will help you travel vicariously to all of America's new cocktail capitals. We hope you enjoy the trip!

Dana Cowin
Editor in Chief
FOOD & WINE Magazine

Jim Meehan
Deputy Editor
FOOD & WINE Cocktails 2013

1 MARTINI
A stemmed glass for cocktails served straight up (mixed with ice and then strained).

2 ROCKS
A short glass for spirits served neat (without ice) and drinks over ice. **SINGLE ROCKS** glasses hold up to 6 ounces; double rocks glasses hold closer to 12 ounces.

3 COLLINS
A very tall, narrow glass often used for drinks that are served on ice and topped with soda.

4 WINEGLASS
White wine glasses are a fine substitute for highball glasses and are also good for frozen drinks. Balloon-shaped red wine glasses are ideal for fruity cocktails as well as punches.

5 HIGHBALL
A tall, narrow glass that helps preserve the fizz in drinks served with ice and topped with club soda or tonic water.

6 COUPE
A shallow, wide-mouthed, stemmed glass primarily for small (short) and potent cocktails that are served straight up.

7 PILSNER

A tall, flared glass designed for beer. It's also useful for serving oversize cocktails on ice or drinks with multiple garnishes.

8 HEATPROOF MUG

A durable ceramic or glass cup with a handle. Perfect for coffee spiked with whiskey or other spirits as well as toddies and other hot drinks.

9 FLUTE

A tall, slender, usually stemmed glass; its narrow shape helps keep cocktails topped with Champagne or sparkling wine effervescent.

10 FIZZ

A narrow glass for soda-topped drinks without ice. Also called a juice glass or Delmonico glass.

TIKI MUG
(NOT PICTURED)

A tall ceramic mug without a handle that's decorated with a tropical or Polynesian-style motif. It's used for serving tiki drinks.

JULEP CUP
(NOT PICTURED)

A short pewter or silver cup designed to keep juleps (minty, crushed-ice cocktails) cold.

HOME BAR TOOLS

1 ICE PICK
A sharp metal tool with a sturdy handle used to break off chunks from a larger block of ice.

2 BAR SPOON
A long-handled metal spoon that mixes cocktails without creating air bubbles. Also useful to measure small amounts.

3 Y PEELER
A wide peeler that's great for making large and small twists from citrus-fruit peels.

4 JULEP STRAINER
The preferred device for straining cocktails from a mixing glass because it fits securely. Fine holes keep ice out of the drink.

5 WAITER'S CORKSCREW
A pocketknife-like tool with a bottle opener. Bartenders favor it over bulkier, more complicated corkscrews.

6 COBBLER SHAKER
The most commonly used shaker, with a metal cup for mixing drinks with ice, a built-in strainer and a fitted top.

7 ATOMIZER
A small spray bottle used to coat an empty glass with aromatic liquid, such as absinthe, instead of rinsing the glass. Atomizers are sold at beauty-supply stores.

8 HAWTHORNE STRAINER
The best all-purpose strainer. A semicircular spring ensures a spill-proof fit on a shaker. Look for a tightly coiled spring, which keeps muddled fruit and herbs out of drinks.

9 CITRUS JUICER
A metal or ceramic press that allows you to squeeze citrus fruit when you need it.

10 BOSTON SHAKER
The bartender's choice; consists of a mixing glass, usually a pint glass, with a metal canister that covers the glass to create a seal. Shake drinks with the metal half pointing away from you.

11 JAPANESE MIXING GLASS
A heavy, often etched glass that's used for stirring. Its spout makes for graceful pouring.

12 JIGGER
A two-sided stainless measuring instrument for precise mixing.

13 MICROPLANE
A fine-toothed metal grater used for shaving citrus zest and ginger. Small box graters are best for hard spices like nutmeg and cinnamon.

14 MUDDLER
A sturdy tool for crushing herbs and fresh fruit; it's traditionally made of wood. Choose a muddler that can reach the bottom of a shaker; in a pinch, use a long-handled wooden spoon.

15 FINE STRAINER
A fine-mesh strainer set over a glass before the cocktail is poured in (see Fine-Straining Drinks on **P.21**). It keeps bits of muddled herbs, fruit and crushed ice out of drinks.

ESSENTIAL SPIRITS

Mixologists are using just about everything they can get their hands on in their drinks, but these 11 choices are still the backbone of a great cocktail list.

APERITIFS (WINE-BASED)

The word "aperitif" is often used to refer to any predinner drink, but aperitifs are also a category of beverages: light, dry and low-proof, with characteristic bitter flavors. A century ago, mixologists began adding wine-based aperitifs to cocktails instead of simply serving them on their own. Wine-based aperitifs include dry vermouths, **ABOVE,** and their relatives quinquinas (or kinas), such as Lillet and Dubonnet. These contain quinine, a bitter extract from cinnamon-like cinchona bark.

APERITIFS (SPIRIT-BASED)

Low-proof, bitter, spirit-based aperitifs like Campari have always been popular in Europe. Now they're beloved in the US thanks to mixologists' embrace of bottles like Aperol, the bitter orange Italian *aperitivo,* **ABOVE.** Other examples of spirit-based aperitifs are Suze, which is flavored with bitter gentian root; and Cynar, which is made from 13 herbs and plants, including artichokes.

ABSINTHE

An herbal spirit, absinthe was banned in the US in 1912 in part because a key ingredient, wormwood, was thought to be toxic in large doses. In 2007 scientists concluded that modern bottlings are safe. High-quality absinthe is made much like gin: A neutral spirit is infused with botanicals such as fennel seed and anise. The distilled spirit can be either clear (blanche) or green (verte, **ABOVE**). Absinthe is often used in cocktails, as a rinse for a glass or splashed on top of a drink before serving.

VODKA

Produced all over the world, vodka is traditionally distilled from fermented grain or potatoes, but nearly any fruit or vegetable can be used, from grapes to beets. Most flavored vodkas are created by adding ingredients to a neutral spirit; the best are made by macerating citrus, berries or herbs in high-proof neutral alcohol. Aquavit is produced from a neutral alcohol and botanicals like caraway, citrus peel and star anise. Some are barrel-aged after distillation.

GIN

Gin is made by distilling a neutral grain spirit with botanicals such as juniper, coriander and citrus peels. The most ubiquitous style is London dry, **ABOVE**. It's bolder in flavor than the slightly sweet Old Tom gin, an 18th-century style of British gin. Two other types of the spirit are Plymouth, the British Royal Navy's preferred gin for nearly two centuries; and New Western gins, such as Hendrick's, which incorporate unusual botanicals like rose petals. Genever is a botanically rich, clear, malted grain–based spirit.

TEQUILA

The best tequila is made from 100 percent blue agave that is harvested by hand, slow-roasted in ovens, fermented with natural yeast, then distilled. Blanco (white) tequila is unaged. Reposado (rested) tequila, **ABOVE,** ages up to one year in barrels. Añejo (aged) tequila must be aged between one and three years. Mezcal is known for its smoky flavor, which comes from roasting the agave in earthen pits; the finest mezcals are unaged.

RUM

Distilled from cane syrup, molasses or fresh pressed sugarcane, rums are typically produced in tropical regions. White, a.k.a. silver or light, rums can be aged in wood for a short time. Amber (or gold) rum, **ABOVE,** is often aged in oak barrels for a short time; caramel is sometimes added for color. Dark rum is made with molasses; spiced rum is flavored with ingredients such as coconut, vanilla and cinnamon; and rhum agricole and cachaça are distilled from fresh sugarcane juice.

WHISKEY

Whiskey is distilled from a fermented mash of grains such as malted barley, corn, rye or wheat and then matured in oak barrels (except for white whiskey). Scotland and Japan are famous for their single-malt whiskies (produced from 100 percent malted barley from one distillery). Canada favors blended whiskies high in rye. America is known for its corn-based bourbon, robust rye and unaged white whiskeys. Irish whiskey, **ABOVE,** tend to be mellow blends.

BRANDY

Brandies are distilled from a fermented mash of fruit. The best-known brandies are pot-distilled from wines that spend a long time in oak barrels before bottling. French brandies like Armagnac and Cognac, **ABOVE,** are named after the regions where they are made. Other styles include pisco, a spirit distilled from aromatic grapes in Peru and Chile; and eau-de-vie, a specialty of the European Alps, distilled from a fermented mash of ripe fruit such as plums and pears and bottled without aging.

AMARI

Amari ("bitters" in Italian) are bittersweet sipping spirits made by infusing or distilling a neutral spirit with herbs, spices, citrus peels or nuts before sweetening and bottling. Traditionally served after dinner to aid digestion, amari like Averna, Montenegro and Nonino, **ABOVE,** are popular with American bartenders for the complexity and balance they add to cocktails.

LIQUEURS

Among the oldest spirits, liqueurs are produced from a base alcohol that's distilled or macerated with a variety of ingredients and then sweetened. Sugar makes up to 35 percent of a liqueur's weight by volume, and up to 40 percent for crèmes. Liqueurs can be herbal (Chartreuse); citrus- or fruit-based (Cointreau); floral (violet-inflected parfait amour, **ABOVE**); or nut- or seed-based (Frangelico).

BAR LEXICON

AGAVE NECTAR A rich, sweet syrup made from the sap of the cactus-like agave plant.

ALLSPICE DRAM Also known as pimento dram; a rum-based liqueur infused with Jamaican allspice berries. **St. Elizabeth** and **The Bitter Truth** are good brands.

APEROL A vibrant orange-red, low-proof Italian aperitif flavored with bitter orange, rhubarb, gentian and cinchona bark.

BÄRENJÄGER A subtly sweet, honey-flavored German liqueur.

BAROLO CHINATO A Nebbiolo-based fortified wine (produced in Piedmont's Barolo zone) infused with cinchona bark (*china* in Italian) and various roots, herbs and spices, including rhubarb and cardamom.

BATAVIA-ARRACK VAN OOSTEN A clear, spicy and citrusy rum-like spirit made in Java from sugarcane and fermented red rice.

BÉNÉDICTINE An herbal liqueur with flavors of hyssop, angelica, juniper and myrrh. According to legend, the recipe was developed by a French monk in 1510.

BITTERS A concentrated tincture of bitter and aromatic herbs, roots and spices that adds complexity to drinks. Varieties include orange, grapefruit, cherry and aromatic bitters, the best known of which is **Angostura,** created in 1824. **Bittermens** makes bitters in unusual flavors like Xocolatl Mole and Hellfire Habanero Shrub. **Fee Brothers** bitters come in

15 flavors and have been made in Rochester, New York, since the 1950s. **Peychaud's** bitters have flavors of anise and cherry; the recipe dates to 19th-century New Orleans.

BONAL GENTIANE-QUINA A slightly bitter French aperitif wine infused with gentian root and cinchona bark, the source of quinine.

BONDED WHISKEY A whiskey that's been produced by a single distillery, distilled during a single season, aged a minimum of four years, bottled at 100 proof and stored in a "bonded" warehouse under US government supervision.

BRANCA MENTA A spin-off of the bitter Italian digestif Fernet-Branca (**P.18**) with a pronounced peppermint and menthol flavor.

BYRRH GRAND QUINQUINA A mildly bitter French aperitif that combines red wine and lightly fermented grape juice with quinine-rich cinchona bark, bitter orange, coffee, cocoa and botanicals.

CAMPARI A potent, bright red Italian aperitif with a bitter orange flavor. It's made from fruit, herbs and spices.

CARPANO ANTICA FORMULA A rich and complex sweet red vermouth from Italy.

CHARTREUSE A spicy herbal French liqueur made from more than 100 botanicals; **green** Chartreuse is more potent than the honey-sweetened **yellow** one.

COCCHI AMERICANO A low-alcohol, white-wine-based Italian aperitif infused with cinchona bark, citrus peels and herbs such as gentian.

COCCHI VERMOUTH DI TORINO A slightly bitter, Moscato-based red vermouth from Italy with hints of citrus, rhubarb and cocoa.

COINTREAU A French triple sec that is made by macerating and distilling sun-dried sweet and bitter orange peels.

CURAÇAO A general term for orange-flavored liqueurs historically produced in the French West Indies.

CYNAR A pleasantly bitter Italian aperitif made from 13 herbs and plants, including artichokes.

DRAMBUIE A whisky-based Scottish liqueur flavored with honey, herbs and spices.

FERNET-BRANCA A potent, bitter-flavored Italian digestif that's made from 27 herbs.

GALLIANO A golden Italian liqueur that includes some 30 herbs and spices, including lavender, anise, star anise, juniper and vanilla.

GRENADINE A sweet red syrup made from a mix of pomegranate juice and sugar (for a Homemade Grenadine recipe, see **P.22**).

HEERING CHERRY LIQUEUR A crimson-colored cherry liqueur made in Denmark since 1818. Heering is drier and more complex than other cherry liqueurs.

KINA L'AVION D'OR A deep golden Swiss aperitif made by infusing white wine with cinchona bark, orange peel, wormwood and spices.

KRONAN SWEDISH PUNSCH A sweet liqueur created from sugarcane spirits including Batavia-Arrack van Oosten (**P.16**).

LICOR 43 A sweet Spanish liqueur with citrus and vanilla flavors.

LILLET A wine-based French aperitif flavored with orange peel and quinine. The **rouge** variety is sweeter than the **blanc.** The **rosé,** made from a blend of the red and white, has a slightly fruity flavor.

MARASCHINO LIQUEUR
A colorless Italian liqueur. The best brands are distilled from sour marasca cherries and their pits, then aged in ash wood vats and sweetened with sugar.

ORGEAT A sweet, non-alcoholic syrup made from almonds or almond extract, sugar and rose or orange flower water.

OVERPROOF RUM Any rum that contains over 60 percent alcohol.

PIMM'S NO. 1 A gin-based English aperitif often served with ginger beer, 7-Up or lemonade.

PINEAU DES CHARENTES A barrel-aged French aperitif produced from unfermented grape juice and young Cognac.

PORT A fortified wine from the Douro region of Portugal. Styles include fruity, young **ruby** port; richer, nuttier **tawny;** and thick-textured, oak-aged **late bottled vintage (LBV).**

SALERS A bittersweet, pale amber French aperitif made predominantly from gentian root.

ST-GERMAIN A French liqueur created by blending macerated elderflower blossoms with eau-de-vie. It has hints of pear, peach and grapefruit zest.

SUZE A bittersweet, aromatic yellow aperitif made from gentian root with hints of vanilla, candied orange and spice.

TRIPLE SEC An orange-flavored liqueur that is similar to curaçao but not as sweet. **Cointreau,** created in 1875, is the most famous. **Combier,** created in 1834, claims to be the world's first.

VS Cognacs labeled VS (Very Special) are aged at least two years. **VSOP** (Very Superior Old Pale) Cognacs must be aged at least four years.

ZWACK An intense Hungarian herbal liqueur made since 1790 from a secret blend of more than 40 herbs and spices.

MIXOLOGY BASICS

MAKING A TWIST

A twist—a small piece of citrus zest—lends a drink concentrated citrus flavor from the peel's essential oils.

TO MAKE AND USE A STANDARD TWIST

1. Use a sharp paring knife or Y peeler to cut a thin, oval, quarter-size disk of the peel, avoiding the pith.

2. Grasp the outer edges skin side down and pinch the twist over the drink. Rub it around the glass rim, then drop it in.

TO MAKE A SPIRAL-CUT TWIST

1. Use a channel knife to cut a 3-inch-long piece of peel with some of the pith intact. Cut the twist over the glass so its essential oils fall into the drink.

2. Wrap the twist around a straw; tighten at both ends to create a curlicue shape.

FLAMING A TWIST

Flaming a lemon or orange twist caramelizes the zest's essential oils.

1. Make a standard twist. Gently grasp the outer edges, skin side down, between the thumb and two fingers and hold it about 4 inches over the cocktail.

2. Hold a lit match over the drink an inch away from the twist—don't let the flame touch the peel—then pinch the edges of the twist sharply so that the citrus oil falls through the flame and into the drink.

SMACKING HERBS

To accentuate the aroma of fresh herbs used for garnish, clap them between your hands over the glass to release the essential oils into the drink.

PERFECTING ICE

The right ice is essential to preparing a balanced and attractive drink.

TO MAKE BIG BLOCKS OF ICE FOR PUNCH BOWLS, pour water into a large, shallow plastic container and freeze. To unmold, first warm the bottom of the container in hot water.

TO MAKE LARGE ICE CUBES FOR ROCKS GLASSES, use flexible silicone ice molds (available at *cocktailkingdom.com*). Or make a large block of ice in a loaf pan and use an ice pick to break off chunks the size you want.

TO MAKE CRUSHED ICE, cover cubes in a clean kitchen towel and pound with a wooden mallet or rolling pin.

TO MAKE CRACKED ICE, place an ice cube in the palm of your hand and tap it with the back of a bar spoon until it breaks into pieces.

TO MAKE CLEAR CUBES, fill ice trays with hot filtered water.

TO MAKE PERFECTLY SQUARE CUBES, use flexible silicone Perfect Cube ice trays (available at *surlatable.com*).

RIMMING A GLASS

1. Spread salt (preferably kosher), sugar or other powdered ingredient on a plate. **2.** Moisten the outer rim of the glass with a citrus-fruit wedge, water or a syrup; roll the outer rim on the plate until it is lightly coated, then tap to release any excess.

FINE-STRAINING DRINKS

To remove tiny fruit or herb particles: **1.** Set a fine strainer over a serving glass. **2.** Make the drink in a shaker or mixing glass, set a julep or Hawthorne strainer (**PP.10** and **11**) on top, then pour through both strainers into the serving glass.

TRENDS

instant cocktails

Long waits for handcrafted cocktails are over. Mixologists are serving premade drinks that have been barrel-aged, bottled or kegged. Cocktails in kegs are dispensed from a tap, like the Roy and Rye (fruit-and-herb-infused rye whiskey) at San Diego's Polite Provisions.

hotel bars

Some of the most legendary bars of the 1900s golden age were in hotel lobbies. Today places like The NoMad in New York City and Bellocq in New Orleans's Hotel Modern are among the chicest hangouts in the nation.

fly-over cocktail capitals

San Francisco and New York, the country's traditional drink meccas, are facing competition from the middle of America, now that groundbreaking cocktail programs are appearing in cities like Denver, Nashville and Louisville.

super-savory drinks

There's almost no ingredient that you won't find in a well-made cocktail these days. San Francisco mixologist Mathias Simonis's unconventional Caprese Daiquiri (**P.91**) is a surprisingly delicious re-creation of the classic Italian salad, including herbed olive oil and a mozzarella ball. Chef Bryan Voltaggio uses "beef ice" made from veal consommé in his cocktails at Range in Washington, DC.

the egg

Frothy egg white foam is key to the silky texture and frothy head of many classic cocktails. Mixologists are playing with the froth, using it as a canvas for creative bitters designs. Bars like Justice Snow's in Aspen, Colorado, are also experimenting with different kinds of eggs; they use quail eggs in their Antarctique cocktail (cachaça, vermouth, St-Germain elderflower liqueur and pineapple juice).

HOMEMADE MIXERS

SIMPLE SYRUP
MAKES ABOUT 12 OUNCES

In a small saucepan, combine 8 ounces water and 1 cup sugar and bring to a boil. Simmer over moderate heat, stirring frequently, until the sugar dissolves, about 3 minutes. Remove from the heat and let cool. Transfer the syrup to a bottle or tightly covered glass jar and refrigerate for up to 1 month.

RICH SIMPLE SYRUP
MAKES ABOUT 8 OUNCES

In a small saucepan, combine 4 ounces water and 1 cup demerara or other raw sugar and bring to a boil. Simmer over moderate heat, stirring, until the sugar dissolves, about 3 minutes. Remove from the heat and let cool. Transfer the syrup to a bottle or tightly covered glass jar and refrigerate for up to 1 month.

VANILLA SIMPLE SYRUP
MAKES ABOUT 12 OUNCES

In a small saucepan, combine 8 ounces water, 1 cup sugar and ½ split vanilla bean and bring to a boil. Simmer over moderate heat, stirring, until the sugar dissolves, about 3 minutes. Let cool, then strain the syrup into a bottle or tightly covered glass jar and refrigerate for up to 1 month.

EASIEST SIMPLE SYRUP
MAKES ABOUT 12 OUNCES

In a bottle or jar with a tight-fitting lid, combine 8 ounces hot water with 1 cup superfine sugar and shake until the sugar dissolves. Let cool, then refrigerate the syrup for up to 1 month.

HOMEMADE GRENADINE
MAKES ABOUT 12 OUNCES

In a bottle or jar with a tight-fitting lid, shake 8 ounces unsweetened pomegranate juice with 1 cup sugar until the sugar dissolves. If desired, add ⅛ teaspoon orange flower water. Refrigerate the grenadine for up to 2 weeks.

a word on honey and agave

Natural sweeteners like honey and agave nectar impart a more complex flavor than simple syrup. To make a pourable syrup, mix two parts warm honey or agave nectar with one part water. (For a less rich syrup, use a 1:1 ratio.) Or simply shake the sweetener and hot water in a jar. Let the syrup cool before using.

For recipes that call for honey syrup, bottle 8 to 12 ounces of honey syrup and keep it in the refrigerator. It's easier than preparing a portion for each serving.

CONVERSION CHART

THE MEASURES FOR SPIRITS AND OTHER LIQUIDS ARE GIVEN IN FLUID OUNCES. REFER TO THE CHART BELOW FOR CONVERSIONS.

CUP	OUNCE	TBSP	TSP
1 c	8 fl oz		
¾ c	6 fl oz		
⅔ c	5⅓ fl oz		
	5 fl oz	10 tbsp	
½ c	4 fl oz		
	3 fl oz	6 tbsp	
⅓ c	2⅔ fl oz		
¼ c	2 fl oz		
	1 fl oz	2 tbsp	
	½ fl oz	1 tbsp	3 tsp
	⅓ fl oz	⅔ tbsp	2 tsp
	¼ fl oz	½ tbsp	1½ tsp

1 OUNCE = ABOUT 32 DASHES   1 DASH = 4 TO 5 DROPS

UFFIZI **P.26**

*"Stone Collection" whiskey glasses
by Jiří Pelcl from Unica Home.*

APERITIFS

INKS BY:

LL THOMPSON • DRINK • BOSTON

AN HOARD • TEARDROP COCKTAIL LOUNGE • PORTLAND, OREGON

A KOPLOWITZ & NICHOLAS KOSEVICH • EAT STREET SOCIAL • MILWAUKEE

AXWELL BRITTEN • MAISON PREMIERE • BROOKLYN, NEW YORK

MOTHER HANDSOME'S PINEAU COBBLER

This refreshing cocktail from Will Thompson of Drink in Boston is filled with chunks of fresh cantaloupe. It pays homage to Mother Handsome, a 19th-century Michigan innkeeper. Her name was perversely affectionate in the same way that calling a big guy "Tiny" is.

Four 1-inch cubes of cantaloupe
3 ounces Pineau des Charentes (Cognac-fortified grape juice)
½ orange wheel
Ice

In a cocktail shaker, lightly muddle the cantaloupe with the Pineau des Charentes and orange. Fill the shaker with ice and shake well. Pour (don't strain) into a chilled white wine glass and serve with a cocktail pick for spearing the cantaloupe chunks. —*Will Thompson*

UFFIZI

📷 PAGE 25

This cocktail is a lighter take on the Salty Dog, the time-honored mix of vodka and grapefruit juice in a salt-rimmed glass. It's made with two kinds of aperitif (drinks with bitter flavors designed to spark the appetite): quinine-infused Bonal and citrusy, bittersweet Cocchi Americano.

1 grapefruit wedge and kosher salt
1½ ounces Bonal Gentiane-Quina
1½ ounces Cocchi Americano
2 ounces fresh white grapefruit juice
Cracked ice

Moisten the outer rim of a chilled double rocks glass with the grapefruit wedge and coat lightly with salt. Add the Bonal, Cocchi Americano and grapefruit juice, then fill the glass with cracked ice and stir well. —*WT*

MOTHER HANDSOME'S
PINEAU COBBLER

"Claire" goblet by William Yeoward.

LITTLE VALIANT

Instead of mixing salt with the other ingredients, Thompson sprinkles it on the large ice cube in the cocktail. As the salt melts through the ice, the flavor of the drink changes from bitter to briny.

1 large ice cube (page 20)
2 ounces Lillet blanc
1 ounce gentian aperitif, such as Salers or Suze
¾ teaspoon fresh lemon juice
2 dashes of orange bitters
Small pinch of salt, for garnish

Place the ice cube in a chilled rocks glass. Add all of the remaining ingredients except the garnish and stir well. Sprinkle the salt on the ice. *—Will Thompson*

ROYAL JAMAICA 10 DOWNING STREET

The combination of aperitif wine, funky Jamaican rum and chocolate-flavored crème de cacao makes this drink sweet and pleasantly bitter at the same time.

2 ounces Kina L'Avion d'Or
(slightly bitter aperitif wine)
½ ounce white overproof Jamaican rum
¼ ounce white crème de cacao
Ice
1 grapefruit twist

In a mixing glass, combine the Kina, rum and crème de cacao; fill with ice and stir well. Strain into a chilled coupe. Pinch the grapefruit twist over the drink and discard. *—WT*

LIFE VEST

"A buddy of mine walked into the bar and asked for a cocktail that 'won't get me drunk, because I'm meeting a girl here,'" says Sean Hoard, bar manager of Teardrop Cocktail Lounge in Portland, Oregon. "I put together this low-octane Culross variation and called it a Life Vest because I was trying to save my friend's night."

1 ounce Carpano Antica Formula or other sweet vermouth
1 ounce Cocchi Americano (fortified, slightly bitter aperitif wine)
¾ ounce apricot brandy
½ ounce fresh lemon juice
Ice

In a cocktail shaker, combine the vermouth, Cocchi Americano, brandy and lemon juice. Fill the shaker with ice and shake well. Strain into a chilled coupe. —*Sean Hoard*

ROYAL SUNDAY MORNING*

Since moving back to Portland, Hoard has made Sunday brunch at his parents' house a weekly ritual. He mixes this simple cocktail with ingredients his parents always have on hand (vermouth, grapefruit juice and raspberry preserves), then tops it off with sparkling wine.

*For a mocktail variation, see **P.166**.

2 ounces dry vermouth
¾ ounce fresh grapefruit juice
¾ teaspoon raspberry preserves
Ice
1 ounce chilled dry sparkling wine
½ ounce chilled club soda

In a cocktail shaker, combine the vermouth, grapefruit juice and preserves. Fill the shaker with ice and shake well. Fine-strain (**P.21**) into a chilled coupe and top with the sparkling wine and club soda. —*SH*

MARSEILLE CAN YOU SEE?

Hoard developed this cocktail after drinking pastis during a pétanque tournament. In France, pastis is usually served neat or blended with water. Here, Hoard combines the anise-flavored spirit with three common mixers: vermouth, orange juice and lime juice.

1½ ounces French blanc vermouth, such as Dolin
¼ ounce pastis
½ ounce fresh orange juice
¼ ounce fresh lime juice
Ice cubes, plus crushed ice for serving

In a cocktail shaker, combine the vermouth, pastis and citrus juices. Fill the shaker with ice cubes and shake well. Strain into a chilled rocks glass and top with crushed ice.
—Sean Hoard

SECOND COUSIN

Since dry vermouth is a major component of the Second Cousin, Hoard prefers to use a good-quality brand like Dolin. It's lighter, drier and smoother than less expensive commercial varieties.

¼ ounce absinthe
Ice
1 ounce dry vermouth
1 ounce Cocchi Americano (fortified, slightly bitter aperitif wine)
¼ ounce pear brandy
1 teaspoon honey syrup (⅔ teaspoon honey mixed with ⅓ teaspoon warm water)
1 grapefruit twist

Rinse a chilled rocks glass with the absinthe; pour out the excess and add ice. In a mixing glass, combine the vermouth, Cocchi Americano, pear brandy and honey syrup; fill with ice and stir well. Strain into the prepared rocks glass, then pinch the grapefruit twist over the drink and discard. —SH

SEROTINA

Ira Koplowitz and Nicholas Kosevich of Eat Street Social in Milwaukee make this aromatic cocktail with apricot eau-de-vie. This clear fruit brandy is usually served as a digestif in Europe, but American mixologists like to blend it into cocktails to add concentrated fruit flavor without sweetness.

1 ounce apricot eau-de-vie
½ ounce cherry-vanilla bitters
¾ teaspoon honey
Ice
2 ounces chilled club soda
1 lemon twist, for garnish

In a chilled rocks glass, combine the eau-de-vie, bitters and honey and stir well. Add ice and stir again. Stir in the club soda, then pinch the lemon twist over the drink and drop it in. *—Ira Koplowitz and Nicholas Kosevich*

SUZE BRAMBLE

This drink has the characteristic rich pink hue and sweet-tart flavors of a classic Bramble (gin, blackberries and lemon juice); the complex French gentian aperitif Suze gives it a bitter edge.

¾ ounce Suze
¾ ounce blanco tequila, preferably Chinaco
½ ounce Simple Syrup (page 22)
½ ounce fresh grapefruit juice
¼ ounce fresh lemon juice
2 blackberries
Ice

In a cocktail shaker, combine the Suze, tequila, Simple Syrup, citrus juices and 1 of the blackberries. Fill the shaker with ice and shake well. Fine-strain (**P.21**) into a chilled ice-filled highball glass and garnish with the remaining blackberry. *—IK and NK*

SUZE BRAMBLE
"Cascade" tumbler by Sugahara from Dandelion.

TO HELL WITH SPAIN

The lovely cherry flavors here are from Heering cherry liqueur and Cherry Bark Vanilla bitters from Bittercube, an artisanal bitters company founded by Koplowitz and Kosevich. Instead of rinsing the glass with absinthe and then pouring it out, you can mist it with an atomizer so you don't waste a single drop.

¼ ounce absinthe
1½ ounces Cynar (bitter artichoke aperitif)
¾ ounce bonded rye whiskey,
   such as Rittenhouse Rye 100 proof
¼ ounce Heering cherry liqueur
¼ ounce fresh lemon juice
Dash of cherry-vanilla bitters
Ice

Rinse a chilled coupe with the absinthe; pour out the excess. In a mixing glass, combine the Cynar, whiskey, Heering, lemon juice and bitters; fill with ice and stir well. Strain into the prepared coupe. —*Ira Koplowitz and Nicholas Kosevich*

IN THE BERGAMOT

MAKES 8 SERVINGS

ALLOW 2 HOURS FOR CHILLING

Koplowitz and Kosevich make an easy Earl Grey tea–infused vermouth to add a fragrant citrus flavor to this make-ahead pitcher drink.

3 Earl Grey tea bags
8 ounces Cocchi Vermouth di Torino
   or other sweet vermouth
8 ounces Aperol
8 ounces bourbon
½ ounce orange bitters
Ice
16 ounces chilled club soda
16 orange twists, for garnish

In a bowl, cover 3 Earl Grey tea bags with the vermouth; let steep for 20 minutes, then strain into a pitcher. Stir in the Aperol, bourbon and bitters; refrigerate until chilled, about 2 hours. Stir, then pour into chilled ice-filled collins glasses. Stir in 2 ounces of club soda for each drink and garnish with 2 orange twists. —*IK and NK*

TURN OF THE CENTURY

At Maison Premiere in Brooklyn, New York, Maxwell Britten stocks over two dozen kinds of absinthe. In this variation on the 20th Century cocktail, he uses Kübler, a clear absinthe that turns milky white when mixed with water or ice.

¾ ounce absinthe blanche, such as Kübler
¾ ounce Lillet blanc
¼ ounce white crème de cacao
¾ ounce fresh lemon juice
½ ounce Simple Syrup (page 22)
Ice
1 lemon twist, for garnish

In a cocktail shaker, combine the absinthe, Lillet, crème de cacao, lemon juice and Simple Syrup. Fill the shaker with ice and shake well. Strain into a chilled coupe and garnish with the twist. —*Maxwell Britten*

MAISON PREMIERE ABSINTHE COLADA

Britten serves this absinthe-based piña colada on a saucer, which is an old Parisian way of keeping track of rounds. Prices for the absinthe were painted on the plates, making it easy to tally the bar tab as the saucers stacked up.

¾ ounce absinthe verte, such as Duplais
½ ounce aged rum, preferably Jamaican
1 teaspoon crème de menthe
1 ounce chilled pineapple juice
¾ ounce coconut syrup (see Note)
½ ounce fresh lemon juice
Crushed ice
1 mint sprig, for garnish

In a chilled pilsner glass, combine the absinthe, rum, crème de menthe, pineapple juice, coconut syrup and lemon juice; fill with crushed ice and spin a swizzle stick or bar spoon between your hands to mix the drink. Top with more crushed ice; garnish with the mint sprig. —*MB*
NOTE Coconut syrup is available at *kalustyans.com*.

LADY LIBERTY

Britten likes to use Pacifique green absinthe in this floral and fruity cocktail. Pacific Distillery started making Pacifique in Washington state with a 19th-century French recipe after the US worm-wood absinthe ban was lifted in 2007.

1 ounce absinthe verte, such as Pacifique
1 ounce chilled Sauvignon Blanc
   or other dry white wine
1 ounce French blanc vermouth, such as Dolin
¾ ounce fresh grapefruit juice
½ ounce Simple Syrup (page 22)
Dash of orange flower water
Cracked ice
1 grapefruit twist, for garnish

In a chilled Pontarlier glass (a traditional absinthe glass) or white wine glass, combine all of the ingredients except ice and the garnish. Fill the glass with cracked ice and stir well; garnish with the twist. —*Maxwell Britten*

ABSINTHE JULEP

Juleps (minty, crushed-ice cocktails served in metal julep cups) became such a hit at Maison Premiere that an entire section of the menu is now devoted to them. This mint julep variation swaps absinthe for bourbon and adds blackberry liqueur for a little extra sweetness.

2 mint sprigs
1 sugar cube
1 ounce absinthe verte, such as Lucid
1 teaspoon crème de mûre (blackberry liqueur)
1 ounce cold water
Crushed ice

In a chilled julep cup, muddle 1 of the mint sprigs, then discard. Muddle the sugar cube with the absinthe, crème de mûre and water in the cup and fill with crushed ice. Spin a swizzle stick or bar spoon between your hands to mix the drink. Top with more crushed ice and garnish with the remaining mint sprig.—*MB*

LADY LIBERTY
"Variations" glasses by Patricia
Urquiola for Baccarat.

VODKA

DRINKS BY:

TONY ABOU-GANIM • THE MODERN MIXOLOGIST CONSULTING • LAS VEGAS

JOEL TEITELBAUM • HARRY DENTON'S STARLIGHT ROOM • SAN FRANCISCO

IVY MIX • CLOVER CLUB • BROOKLYN, NEW YORK

KATHY CASEY • KATHY CASEY FOOD STUDIOS • SEATTLE

GARDEN RICKEY **P.51**

Jigger and cocktail picks from Cocktail Kingdom; glass bowl from The End of History; "Chandernagor" glass by Hermès.

THE WIZARD

"The Wizard is a spirit-only, stirred cocktail that celebrates one of my favorite liqueurs, yellow Chartreuse," says Las Vegas–based mixologist Tony Abou-Ganim. He recommends a big, full-bodied potato vodka with a lot of character, such as Chopin.

2 ounces vodka, preferably potato

1 ounce Italian bianco vermouth, such as Cinzano

½ ounce yellow Chartreuse

2 dashes of orange bitters

Ice

1 lemon twist, for garnish

In a mixing glass, combine the vodka, vermouth, Chartreuse and bitters; fill with ice and stir well. Strain into a chilled coupe and garnish with the lemon twist.
—*Tony Abou-Ganim*

SARAH'S SMILE

MAKES 8 SERVINGS

ALLOW 2 HOURS FOR CHILLING

Light and immensely refreshing, Sarah's Smile is a great cocktail for parties because it can be made in large batches and chilled in advance. Abou-Ganim quickly shakes each drink with ice and strains it into a glass. To save time, shake two servings at once.

12 ounces vodka, preferably grape, such as Cîroc

8 ounces St-Germain elderflower liqueur

4 ounces Aperol

8 ounces fresh Ruby Red grapefruit juice

8 ounces fresh lemon juice

4 ounces Simple Syrup (page 22)

Ice

8 Ruby Red grapefruit wheels and 8 mint sprigs, for garnish

In a pitcher, combine all of the ingredients except ice and the garnishes. Refrigerate until chilled, about 2 hours. To serve, fill a shaker with ice. Add a quarter of the punch and shake well. Strain into 2 chilled ice-filled collins glasses and garnish each drink with 1 grapefruit wheel and 1 mint sprig. Repeat with the remaining punch. —*TAG*

THE WIZARD
"Club Stirrer" swizzle stick by Ciovere;
"Crocodile" wallpaper by Brett Design.

BUBBLING MARIO

Abou-Ganim developed this cooler for the Mario Batali Foundation's annual golf tournament. "I went from hole to hole on a golf cart shaking up this drink," he says. With two Italian ingredients— Prosecco and the bright orange-red aperitivo Aperol—the cocktail is a nod to Batali's heritage.

1½ ounces vodka, preferably wheat, such as Russian Standard
¾ ounce Aperol
1 ounce fresh lemon juice
1 ounce fresh orange juice
½ ounce honey syrup (2 teaspoons honey mixed with 1 teaspoon warm water)

Ice

1 ounce chilled Prosecco
1 orange wheel and 1 spiral-cut lemon twist (page 20), for garnish

In a cocktail shaker, combine the vodka, Aperol, lemon juice, orange juice and honey syrup. Fill the shaker with ice and shake well. Strain into a chilled ice-filled collins glass and top with the Prosecco. Garnish with the orange wheel and lemon twist. —*Tony Abou-Ganim*

BLACKBERRY SMASH

Abou-Ganim includes fresh blackberries, a high-quality blackberry liqueur and plenty of mint in his vodka variation on a classic smash.

4 blackberries

9 mint leaves, plus 1 mint sprig dusted with confectioners' sugar for garnish

½ ounce Simple Syrup (page 22)

1½ ounces vodka, preferably mixed-grain, such as Van Gogh

½ ounce blackberry liqueur

1 ounce fresh lemon juice

Ice cubes, plus cracked ice for serving

In a shaker, muddle 2 of the blackberries with the mint leaves and Simple Syrup. Add the vodka, blackberry liqueur, lemon juice and ice cubes; shake well. Fine-strain (**P.21**) into a chilled cracked-ice-filled rocks glass; garnish with 2 blackberries and the mint sprig. —*Tony Abou-Ganim*

CUCUMBER COLLINS

This take on the Tom Collins is from Joel Teitelbaum of Harry Denton's Starlight Room in San Francisco. He mixes vodka with cucumber, lemon juice and fresh mint, then tops the drink with soda water "to finish with that slight carbon dioxide astringency you get from good seltzer," he says.

8 mint leaves

Three ¼-inch-thick cucumber wheels, plus 1 long cucumber slice for garnish

¾ ounce Simple Syrup (page 22)

2 ounces vodka, preferably grape or wheat

1 ounce fresh lemon juice

Ice

1 ounce chilled seltzer

In a shaker, muddle the mint with the 3 cucumber wheels and Simple Syrup. Add the vodka, lemon juice and ice; shake well. Fine-strain (**P.21**) into a chilled ice-filled collins glass, stir in the seltzer and garnish. —*Joel Teitelbaum*

VIEUX BLANC

Vieux Blanc is Teitelbaum's update of the Vieux Carré, an old New Orleans classic. "The Vieux Carré can be intimidating for newly adventurous drinkers," he says. In response to the recent demand for lighter versions of time-honored cocktails, Teitelbaum replaces the original's rye whiskey with rye vodka, which has similar notes of spicy rye.

1½ ounces vodka, preferably rye, such as Bols
¾ ounce pisco
¾ ounce French blanc vermouth, such as Dolin
¼ ounce Galliano (Italian herbal liqueur)
¼ ounce Bénédictine (spiced herbal liqueur)
2 dashes of lemon bitters
Ice
1 lemon twist

In a mixing glass, combine all of the ingredients except ice and the lemon twist; fill with ice and stir well. Strain into a chilled coupe, then pinch the twist over the drink and discard. —JT

SPICED PIMM'S

Teitelbaum spices up a Pimm's Cup with amaro, cinnamon and ginger beer, giving the popular summer drink a cold-weather makeover. "Vodka acts as the silent partner here as the spices mix with fresh lemon," he says.

1½ ounces vodka, preferably grain, such as Skyy
1 ounce Pimm's No. 1 (gin-based English aperitif)
½ ounce Amaro Nonino
   (bittersweet herbal digestif)
1 ounce fresh lemon juice
½ ounce Simple Syrup (page 22)
Ice
1 ounce chilled ginger beer
Pinch of cinnamon, for garnish

In a cocktail shaker, combine the vodka, Pimm's, amaro, lemon juice and Simple Syrup. Fill the shaker with ice and shake well. Strain into a chilled ice-filled highball glass, stir in the ginger beer and garnish with the cinnamon. —JT

BLACK & GOLD*

A dessert of strawberry sorbet with balsamic vinegar gave Teitelbaum the idea for this fruity cocktail with a slight black-pepper kick. Be sure to use a good-quality aged balsamic, which will add a mildly woody flavor because of time spent in the barrel.

For a mocktail variation, see **P.160.*

2　ounces vodka, preferably potato, such as Karlsson's Gold
1　ounce fresh lemon juice
1　ounce Black Pepper Syrup (below)
3　strawberries, quartered
¾　teaspoon aged balsamic vinegar
Ice
1　lemon wheel, for garnish

In a cocktail shaker, combine the vodka, lemon juice, Black Pepper Syrup, strawberries and balsamic vinegar. Fill the shaker with ice and shake well. Fine-strain (**P.21**) into a chilled ice-filled rocks glass and garnish with the lemon wheel. —*Joel Teitelbaum*

BLACK PEPPER SYRUP

In a small saucepan, combine 4 ounces water with ½ cup sugar and ½ cup whole black peppercorns and bring to a boil. Reduce the heat to moderately low and simmer for about 10 minutes. Strain the Black Pepper Syrup into a jar and let cool. Cover and refrigerate for up to 2 weeks. Makes about 3 ounces.

BLACK & GOLD

"Cliff" glass by Nason Moretti from TableArt; Sieger by Furstenberg "Sip of Gold" Champagne cup from Fitzsu.

THORN ROSE ROYAL

Ivy Mix of the Clover Club in Brooklyn, New York, came up with the idea for this cocktail when she made herself some jasmine green tea with ginger and lemon to soothe a cold. She uses her own jasmine tea–infused vodka and tops off the drink with rosé Champagne "to give it an extra sparkle."

1   thin quarter-size slice of fresh ginger
¾   ounce Simple Syrup (page 22)
2   ounces Jasmine Tea–Infused Vodka (below)
½   teaspoon maraschino liqueur
¾   ounce fresh lemon juice
Ice
1½   ounces chilled rosé Champagne or sparkling wine
1   lemon wheel, for garnish

In a cocktail shaker, muddle the ginger with the Simple Syrup. Add the infused vodka, maraschino liqueur and lemon juice. Fill the shaker with ice and shake well. Strain into a chilled ice-filled wineglass, top with the Champagne and garnish with the lemon wheel. —*Ivy Mix*

JASMINE TEA–INFUSED VODKA

In a jar, cover 1 jasmine tea bag with 3 ounces vodka. Let the vodka steep for 10 minutes. Discard the tea bag. Cover and store the infused vodka at room temperature for up to 1 month. Makes 3 ounces.

THORN ROSE ROYAL

*"Gigolo" wineglass by Nason Moretti
from TableArt.*

CIRUELA DE JEREZ

ALLOW 2 DAYS FOR
STEEPING

Inspired by a plum-infused fortified wine she had in Spain, Mix infuses vodka with ripe red plums, then stirs it with light, nutty fino sherry.

2 ounces Red Plum–Infused Vodka (below)
¾ ounce Lillet rosé
¼ ounce fino sherry, preferably Lustau
4 drops of orange flower water
Ice
1 lemon twist, for garnish

In a mixing glass, combine the infused vodka, Lillet, sherry and orange flower water; fill with ice and stir well. Strain into a chilled coupe and garnish with the twist. —*Ivy Mix*

RED PLUM–INFUSED VODKA

In a jar, combine 6 ounces vodka with 1 quartered ripe plum. Cover and let stand at room temperature for 2 days. Pour through a fine strainer into a clean jar and store at room temperature for up to 1 month. Makes 6 ounces.

SECOND LEFT *

"When I visit the West Coast, the fruit bowls are filled with blood oranges all the time," Mix says. Because there's a limited season for the fruit on the East Coast, she uses blood orange marmalade instead, combining it with sherry vinegar to make this cocktail. Buy a good-quality sherry vinegar; cheap ones can taste harsh.

*For a mocktail variation, see P.164.

2 ounces vodka, preferably wheat
¾ ounce fresh lemon juice
1 tablespoon blood orange marmalade
¼ ounce Simple Syrup (page 22)
½ teaspoon sherry vinegar
Ice
1 ounce chilled club soda
1 blood orange wheel, for garnish

In a cocktail shaker, combine the vodka, lemon juice, marmalade, Simple Syrup and vinegar. Fill the shaker with ice and shake well. Strain into a chilled ice-filled collins glass, stir in the club soda and garnish. —*IM*

MOCHELIA

This riff on a White Russian (vodka, coffee liqueur and cream) is upgraded with dark chocolate vodka, vanilla simple syrup and fresh whipped cream. Mix prefers Alchemia chocolate vodka. Made with macerated cocoa nibs, the vodka develops a robust, dark chocolate aroma that's richer than the milk chocolate flavor of other brands.

2 ounces chocolate vodka
¾ ounce coffee liqueur
1 teaspoon Vanilla Simple Syrup (page 22)
Ice
2 ounces chilled heavy cream
Pinch of unsweetened cocoa powder, for garnish

In a mixing glass, combine the vodka, liqueur and Vanilla Simple Syrup; fill with ice and stir well. Strain into a chilled coupe. Shake the cream vigorously in a cocktail shaker until softly whipped. Spoon the cream over the drink and garnish with the cocoa powder. —IM

GARDEN RICKEY

📷 PAGE 39

This herbal take on a traditional cooler called the Rickey (spirit, lime and seltzer) is from Kathy Casey, host of the online cocktail show Kathy Casey's Liquid Kitchen. She combines celery and cucumber with aquavit, a clear Scandinavian spirit flavored with caraway and other botanicals. Casey suggests mixing in locally sourced honey, which lends the cocktail an additional layer of flavor and helps support the "bee'vironment."

Two ½-inch celery rib slices, plus 1 small
    leafy celery rib from the heart for garnish
Three ¼-inch-thick cucumber wheels,
    plus 1 cucumber slice for garnish
1 ounce aquavit
1 ounce gin
¾ ounce fresh lime juice
¾ ounce honey syrup (1 tablespoon honey
    mixed with ½ tablespoon warm water)
Ice
1½ ounces chilled club soda

In a shaker, muddle the 2 celery slices and 3 cucumber wheels. Add the aquavit, gin, lime juice and honey syrup; fill with ice and shake vigorously. Fine-strain (**P.21**) into a chilled ice-filled collins glass, stir in the soda and garnish with the celery rib and cucumber slice. —*Kathy Casey*

CITRUS SCANDI

Casey pairs this drink with raw oysters. She puts a little aquavit in a small mister and spritzes the shucked oysters just before serving them.

1 orange wedge
1½ ounces vodka
¼ ounce aquavit
¼ ounce Cointreau or other triple sec
¾ ounce fresh grapefruit juice
Ice
1 orange twist

Squeeze the orange wedge into a cocktail shaker, drop it in, then add the vodka, aquavit, Cointreau and grapefruit juice. Fill the shaker with ice and shake well. Strain into a chilled coupe or 2 shot glasses; pinch the orange twist over the drink and discard. —*Kathy Casey*

URI

Uri is Casey's Norwegian play on the Manhattan, which she mixes with Linie, an aged aquavit. Matured in oak casks in ships that travel from Norway to Australia and then back again, Linie is thought to develop a richer flavor from sloshing around in the barrels.

2 ounces aged aquavit
1 ounce sweet vermouth
Dash of orange bitters
Ice
3 brandied cherries skewered on a pick, for garnish

In a mixing glass, combine the aquavit, vermouth and bitters. Fill the glass three-quarters full with ice and stir well. Strain into a chilled coupe and garnish with the brandied cherries. —*KC*

CITRUS SCANDI

"Frosted Dot" coupes from BHLDN; "Celeste" cocktail shaker by Ralph Lauren.

JUDY WOODS **P.68**

*"Manhattan" ice bucket and glasses
by Rogaska; "Montgomery" jigger
by Ralph Lauren.*

GIN

TROPICAL HONEY PUNCH

MAKES 8 SERVINGS

ALLOW 2 HOURS FOR CHILLING

"With this punch I wanted to re-create classic tiki flavors," says Erick Castro of Polite Provisions in San Diego. "They highlight the botanicals in the gin and the playful funkiness you can only get from Jamaican rum." The drink's uncommon garnish—a pinch of cinnamon—accents the rum.

8 ounces London dry gin

4 ounces aged rum, preferably Jamaican

4 ounces Velvet Falernum (clove-spiced liqueur)

6 ounces fresh lemon juice

½ cup honey syrup (⅓ cup honey mixed with 2 tablespoons plus 2 teaspoons warm water)

8 dashes of Angostura bitters

1 big block of ice, plus 8 large ice cubes for serving (page 20)

8 ounces chilled sparkling water

8 lemon wheels, 8 pineapple spears and cinnamon, for garnish

In a punch bowl, combine all of the ingredients except the ice, sparkling water and garnishes. Refrigerate the punch until chilled, about 2 hours. Stir the punch well, then add the big block of ice and the sparkling water. Ladle each drink into a chilled rocks glass over 1 large ice cube. Garnish each drink with 1 lemon wheel, 1 pineapple spear and a pinch of cinnamon. —*Erick Castro*

TROPICAL HONEY
PUNCH

*"Relax" glasses by Sugahara
from Dandelion.*

MUSIC BOX

Grapefruit bitters and grapefruit-inflected Sauvignon Blanc bring out the citrus flavor of London dry gin here.

2 ounces London dry gin, such as Beefeater 24
¾ ounce fresh lemon juice
¾ ounce Simple Syrup (page 22)
1 large egg white
2 dashes of grapefruit bitters
Ice
¾ ounce chilled Sauvignon Blanc or other crisp white wine
½ orange wheel, for garnish

In a cocktail shaker, combine the gin, lemon juice, Simple Syrup, egg white and bitters and shake vigorously. Fill the shaker with ice and shake again. Strain into a chilled ice-filled rocks glass, top with the wine and garnish with the orange wheel. —*Erick Castro*

OCEANSIDE

Castro muddles plenty of mint leaves with simple syrup, shakes the drink, then pours it through two strainers to remove any particles. The result is a perfectly silky cocktail.

8 mint leaves
¾ ounce Simple Syrup (page 22)
2 ounces London dry gin
1 ounce fresh lime juice
Dash of celery bitters
Pinch of sea salt
Ice

In a cocktail shaker, muddle 7 of the mint leaves with the Simple Syrup, then add the gin, lime juice, bitters and salt. Fill the shaker with ice and shake well. Fine-strain (**P.21**) into a chilled coupe and garnish with the remaining mint leaf. —EC

BROKEN HALO

A lovely aperitif, the Broken Halo combines Plymouth gin (an aromatic style of the spirit that's fruitier than London dry) and nutty, rich oloroso sherry. "This drink is meant to stimulate the appetite and calm the nerves after a long day at work," Castro says.

1½ ounces Plymouth gin
1½ ounces oloroso sherry
¼ ounce maraschino liqueur
Ice, plus 1 large ice cube (page 20) for serving
1 orange twist, for garnish

In a mixing glass, combine the gin, sherry and maraschino liqueur; fill with ice and stir well. Strain the drink into a chilled rocks glass over the large ice cube and garnish with the orange twist. —EC

CHARTREUSE GIN DAISY

Las Vegas mixologist Patricia Richards swaps honey-sweetened yellow Chartreuse (a spicy herbal liqueur) for the usual grenadine in her simple Gin Daisy variation.

2¼ ounces London dry gin
¼ ounce yellow Chartreuse
¾ ounce fresh lemon juice
¼ ounce agave nectar
Dash of orange bitters
Ice
1 brandied cherry, for garnish

In a cocktail shaker, combine the gin, yellow Chartreuse, lemon juice, agave nectar and orange bitters. Fill the cocktail shaker with ice and shake well. Strain into a chilled martini glass and garnish with the cherry.
—*Patricia Richards*

CHARTREUSE
GIN DAISY

*"Newport" glass by Theresienthal
from TableArt.*

RIVIERA

When Richards set out to create a new aperitif for the Sinatra restaurant at Wynn Las Vegas and Encore Resort, she came up with this lighter, grapefruit-spiked take on the Negroni.

1½ ounces dry vermouth
1 ounce Aperol
¾ ounce London dry gin
1½ ounces fresh Ruby Red grapefruit juice
¼ ounce agave nectar
Ice
¼ Ruby Red grapefruit wheel, for garnish

In a cocktail shaker, combine all of the ingredients except ice and the garnish. Fill the shaker with ice and shake briefly. Strain into a chilled ice-filled double rocks glass and garnish with the grapefruit wheel. —*Patricia Richards*

BASIL GIMLET

This extraordinary twist on the traditional gimlet includes fresh basil and celery bitters. A long-lost type of bitters from the 19th century that has made a comeback in recent years, celery bitters are especially delicious in gin and vodka cocktails.

5 basil leaves, plus 1 small basil sprig for garnish
1 ounce fresh lime juice
2¼ ounces London dry gin, such as Martin Miller's
1 ounce Simple Syrup (page 22)
Drop of celery bitters
Ice

In a cocktail shaker, gently muddle the basil leaves with the lime juice, then add the gin, Simple Syrup and celery bitters. Fill the shaker with ice and shake well. Fine-strain (**P.21**) into a chilled martini glass and garnish with the basil sprig. —*PR*

BASIL GIMLET

"Pebbles" martini glass by Moser; "Atelier" cocktail shaker by Monique Lhuillier for Waterford.

MILLER'S CROSSING

James Wampler of The Gin Joint in Charleston, South Carolina, tried making this drink with many types of gin. "The one that tasted right was Martin Miller's," he says. It's a London dry gin beloved by bartenders for its exceptional silkiness.

2 thin cucumber slices
1 mint leaf
1½ ounces London dry gin
¾ ounce fresh lime juice
½ ounce Simple Syrup (page 22)
Crushed ice

In a cocktail shaker, muddle 1 of the cucumber slices with the mint leaf. Add the gin, lime juice and Simple Syrup and shake without ice. Fine-strain (**P.21**) into a chilled crushed-ice-filled rocks glass and garnish with the remaining cucumber slice. —*James Wampler*

NEWPORT SNAP

"This recipe takes a common gin sour and makes it uncommonly good," says Wampler. It features pink gin (a gin blended with bitters, concocted by Royal Navy men to cure seasickness) and a Pinot Noir float on the top.

2 ounces pink gin, preferably Rogue
¾ ounce Simple Syrup (page 22)
¾ ounce fresh lemon juice
Ice
½ ounce Pinot Noir or other light, fruity red wine

In a cocktail shaker, combine the gin, Simple Syrup and lemon juice. Fill the shaker with ice and shake well. Strain into a chilled ice-filled rocks glass and float the wine on top, slowly pouring it over the back of a bar spoon near the drink's surface. —*JW*

NEWPORT SNAP
"Mixology" glass by Waterford.

ANGEL OF DEATH

Here, Wampler uses Death's Door, a London dry–style gin that he says "creates a wickedly intense cocktail with hints of chocolate." Two kinds of bitters, Angostura and orange, give the drink a wonderful complexity. Use one dash of each, or two if you like your cocktails to have an extra edge.

2 ounces dry gin, such as Death's Door
¾ ounce Carpano Antica Formula
 or other sweet vermouth
¾ ounce Campari
2 dashes each of Angostura and orange bitters
Ice
1 spiral-cut orange twist (page 20), for garnish

In a mixing glass, combine the gin, vermouth, Campari and both bitters; fill with ice and stir well. Strain into a chilled coupe and garnish with the twist. —*James Wampler*

PRIOR'S FIX

Wampler's twist on the Ramos Gin Fizz has a Scotch rinse, a frothy egg white head and a healthy dose of the herbal liqueur Bénédictine. He mixes the drink with a New Western gin, a style with more "botanical democracy" than juniper-heavy London dry. The No. 209 here is a small-batch gin that's peppery, citrusy and ultra-smooth.

¾ teaspoon Islay Scotch
2 ounces New Western gin, such as
 No. 209, or another dry gin
¾ ounce Bénédictine
1 ounce chilled heavy cream
½ ounce Simple Syrup (page 22)
½ ounce fresh lemon juice
½ ounce fresh lime juice
1 large egg white
Ice
2 ounces chilled club soda

Rinse a chilled collins glass with the Scotch; do not pour out the excess. In a cocktail shaker, combine the gin, Bénédictine, cream, Simple Syrup, citrus juices and egg white and shake vigorously; fill with ice and shake again. Pour into the collins glass and top with the soda. —*JW*

ANGEL OF DEATH

JUDY WOODS

📷 PAGE 55

Erin Harris of Jimmy's in Aspen, Colorado, creates this fresh and floral cocktail with Old Tom gin, a lightly sweetened style of the spirit that was popular in the 18th century.

2 ounces Old Tom gin
¾ ounce Aperol
¾ ounce fresh lemon juice
¾ ounce fresh orange juice
¾ ounce fresh grapefruit juice
Ice
1 lemon wheel and 1 grapefruit twist, for garnish

In a cocktail shaker, combine the gin, Aperol and citrus juices. Fill the shaker with ice and shake well. Strain into a chilled ice-filled collins glass and garnish with the lemon wheel and grapefruit twist. —*Erin Harris*

M-80

For her riff on the standard French 75 (gin, Champagne, lemon juice and sugar), Harris uses Amaro Montenegro, a light, bittersweet herbal digestif with hints of orange. Prosecco stands in for the Champagne in the classic.

2 ounces barrel-aged Old Tom gin
½ ounce Amaro Montenegro
1 ounce fresh lemon juice
½ ounce Simple Syrup (page 22)
Ice
1 ounce chilled Prosecco
1 lemon twist, for garnish

In a cocktail shaker, combine the gin, amaro, lemon juice and Simple Syrup. Fill the shaker with ice and shake well. Strain into a chilled coupe, top with the Prosecco and garnish with the lemon twist. —*EH*

GENEVER EN FUEGO

This super-smoky drink combines fiery mezcal with genever, a malty, juniper-flavored spirit also known as Holland gin. Honey, lemon and lime give the cocktail a sweet-tart kick.

1½ ounces genever
¾ ounce mezcal
½ ounce fresh lemon juice
½ ounce fresh lime juice
½ ounce honey syrup (2 teaspoons honey mixed with 1 teaspoon warm water)
Ice, plus 1 large ice cube (page 20) for serving

In a cocktail shaker, combine the genever, mezcal, lemon juice, lime juice and honey syrup. Fill the shaker with ice and shake well. Fine-strain (**P.21**) into a chilled double rocks glass over the large ice cube. —EH

TEQUILA

DRINKS BY:

BOBBY HEUGEL • ANVIL BAR & REFUGE • HOUSTON

JULIAN COX • SOIGNÉ GROUP CONSULTING • LOS ANGELES

FRANÇOIS VERA • HARVARD & STONE • LOS ANGELES

LEO ROBITSCHEK • ELEVEN MADISON PARK AND NOMAD • NEW YORK CITY

TAHONA NEGRONY P.75

*"Mixology" coupes from Waterford;
"Arabella" tray by Ralph Lauren.*

CORTEZ JULEP

"I don't think there's a better combination in the cocktail world than tequila and sherry," says Bobby Heugel of Anvil Bar & Refuge in Houston. He recommends using a bold tequila (such as 7 Leguas Blanco) for this nutty sherry–accented drink.

12   mint leaves, plus 1 mint sprig for garnish
1¼   ounces blanco tequila
½   ounce oloroso sherry
½   ounce Cocchi Americano
     (fortified, slightly bitter aperitif wine)
¾   teaspoon Simple Syrup (page 22)
Dash of Angostura bitters
Dash of orange bitters
Crushed ice
  1   blackberry, for garnish

In a chilled julep cup, muddle the mint leaves. Add the tequila, sherry, Cocchi Americano, Simple Syrup and both bitters; fill with crushed ice and mix by spinning a swizzle stick or bar spoon between your hands. Top with more crushed ice and garnish with the blackberry. Lightly crush the mint sprig with your fingers to release the oils, then add it to the cup as garnish. Serve with a metal spoon-straw. —*Bobby Heugel*

CORTEZ JULEP

Nickel julep cups and julep spoon-straw from Cocktail Kingdom.

LA CAPILLA

ALLOW 2 DAYS FOR
INFUSING

La Capilla is a small bar in the town of Tequila, Mexico, where owner Don Javier Delgado Corona first mixed a legendary highball of tequila, lime, salt and cola in 1961. Heugel reinterprets that recipe with blanco tequila ("white" tequila aged for up to two months). He also adds red vermouth that he infuses with cola nuts, the bitter, caffeinated nuts used in the namesake soft drink.

- 2 ounces blanco tequila
- ¾ ounce fresh lime juice
- ¾ ounce Simple Syrup (page 22)
- Ice
- 1½ ounces Cola Nut Vermouth (below)
- 1 lemon wedge, for garnish

In a cocktail shaker, combine the tequila, lime juice and Simple Syrup. Fill the shaker with ice and shake well. Strain into a chilled ice-filled collins glass and top with the Cola Nut Vermouth. Garnish with the lemon wedge.
—*Bobby Heugel*

COLA NUT VERMOUTH

In a jar, combine ⅓ cup cola nuts (available at specialty spice shops and *alibaba.com*) and 6 ounces sweet vermouth, preferably Dolin rouge. Cover and let stand at room temperature for 2 days. Strain the infused vermouth into a clean jar, cover and store at room temperature for up to 2 weeks. Makes 6 ounces.

COLONIA ROMA

The description for Colonia Roma on Anvil Bar's drinks list says, "Don't know what Branca Menta is? Please, ask your bartender before you order this drink. You're welcome." Branca Menta is a digestif with a strong minty-menthol flavor that people either love or hate.

1½ ounces blanco tequila
1½ ounces dry vermouth
½ ounce yellow Chartreuse
½ ounce Branca Menta
½ ounce fresh lime juice
¾ teaspoon Simple Syrup (page 22)
Ice
1 grapefruit twist, for garnish

In a cocktail shaker, combine all of the ingredients except ice and the garnish. Fill the shaker with ice and shake well. Strain into a chilled coupe and garnish with the twist. —*BH*

TAHONA NEGRONY

📷 PAGE 70

ALLOW 3 DAYS FOR INFUSING

For his riff on the three-ingredient Negroni, Heugel swaps blanco tequila for the usual gin and the mildly bitter Italian aperitif Aperol for Campari.

1½ ounces blanco tequila
1 ounce Kronan Swedish *punsch* (spicy, citrusy rum-based spirit)
¾ ounce Clove Aperol (below)
Ice
1 orange twist studded with cloves, for garnish

In a mixing glass, combine the tequila, *punsch* and Clove Aperol; fill with ice and stir well. Strain into a chilled coupe and garnish with the clove-studded orange twist. —*BH*

CLOVE APEROL

In a jar, combine 4 whole cloves and 6 ounces Aperol. Cover and let stand at room temperature for 3 days. Strain the infused Aperol into a clean jar, cover and store at room temperature for up to 2 weeks. Makes 6 ounces.

PALOMA ITALIANA

At the southern Italian restaurant Sotto in Beverly Hills, mixologist Julian Cox uses reposado tequila ("rested," barrel-aged tequila) for this cocktail. It's a variation on the Paloma, made with tequila and grapefruit soda. "I put this drink on the menu as a joke, trying to make it Italian by adding Campari and Italian orange soda," he says. "It became Sotto's most popular drink."

1½ ounces reposado tequila
¾ ounce Campari
¾ ounce fresh pink grapefruit juice
½ ounce fresh lime juice
½ ounce fresh lemon juice
½ ounce agave nectar
Ice
2 ounces chilled Italian orange soda, such as San Pellegrino Aranciata
Pinch of kosher salt
1 spiral-cut grapefruit twist (page 20), for garnish

In a cocktail shaker, combine the tequila, Campari, citrus juices and agave nectar. Fill the shaker with ice and shake well. Add the orange soda and strain into a chilled ice-filled collins or highball glass. Add the salt and garnish with the grapefruit twist. —*Julian Cox*

ANDALUSION

Cox created three versions of this cocktail for Playa in Hollywood: a before-dinner drink mixed with dry fino sherry; one mixed with rich amontillado sherry to drink with dinner; and an after-dinner drink, the Andalusion, that he mixes with sweet sherry.

¾ ounce reposado tequila
¾ ounce Cocchi Americano (fortified, slightly bitter aperitif wine)
¾ ounce Lustau East India Solera sherry
¾ ounce bianco vermouth, preferably Perucchi
Ice
1 lemon twist, for garnish

In a mixing glass, combine the tequila, Cocchi Americano, sherry and vermouth; fill with ice and stir well. Strain into a chilled coupe and garnish with the twist. —*JC*

PALOMA ITALIANA
"Bullet" highball glass from
LSA International.

LUCHADOR'S LADY *

This cocktail gets its gorgeous ruby-red color and a tart, tannic bite from hibiscus tea (available in tea bags, or as dried flowers in Latin markets). Use leftover pineapple syrup to drizzle over ice cream or mix into a boozy shake spiked with rum or tequila.

** For a mocktail variation, see **P.163.***

1½ ounces reposado tequila
1 large egg white
1 ounce chilled brewed hibiscus tea
¾ ounce Caramelized-Pineapple Syrup (below)
½ ounce fresh lime juice
Ice
2 dashes of Peychaud's bitters and a pinch of cinnamon, for garnish

In a cocktail shaker, combine the tequila, egg white, hibiscus tea, Caramelized-Pineapple Syrup and lime juice and shake vigorously. Add ice and shake again. Strain into a chilled rocks glass and garnish with the bitters and cinnamon. —*Julian Cox*

CARAMELIZED-PINEAPPLE SYRUP

In a small skillet, toast ½ cinnamon stick until fragrant. In a small saucepan, combine 1 cup sugar, 4 ounces water, ¼ split vanilla bean and the toasted cinnamon. Cook without stirring until a light amber caramel forms, about 5 minutes. Reduce the heat and add 2½ cups chopped fresh pineapple. Simmer over moderately low heat until the pineapple softens, about 8 minutes. Discard the cinnamon stick and vanilla bean. Let the pineapple mixture cool slightly, then carefully pour into a blender and puree until smooth. Strain the syrup into a jar and let cool. Cover and refrigerate for up to 2 weeks. Makes about 8 ounces.

POBLANO ESCOBAR

Cox muddles pineapple chunks with poblano chiles, which add slight heat, and an unexpected ingredient: cumin. "Combier is a must in the drink," he says. Lighter and slightly drier than other orange liqueurs and triple secs, Combier claims to be the world's first triple sec.

Four ¼-inch-thick rings of poblano chile
Four 1-inch chunks of fresh pineapple
Small pinch of ground cumin
1 ounce reposado tequila, preferably 7 Leguas
1 ounce mezcal
¾ ounce triple sec, preferably Combier
1 ounce fresh lemon juice
½ ounce agave nectar
Ice
1 orange wheel, for garnish

In a cocktail shaker, muddle 3 of the poblano chile rings with the pineapple and cumin. Add the tequila, mezcal, triple sec, lemon juice and agave nectar. Fill the shaker with ice and shake well. Fine-strain (**P.21**) the drink into a chilled ice-filled rocks glass and garnish with the remaining poblano chile ring and the orange wheel. —*JC*

BARELA NO. 2

Before working at Harvard & Stone, François Vera mixed craft cocktails at Cole's, the oldest bar in L.A. This cocktail made with añejo ("aged") tequila, mezcal and sweet vermouth is an ode to Jimmy Barela, who worked as a bartender at Cole's for 65 years.

¼ ounce mezcal
1 long orange peel, for garnish
2 ounces añejo tequila, preferably Chinaco
1 ounce Carpano Antica Formula
3 dashes of orange bitters
Ice

Rinse a chilled rocks glass with the mezcal; pour out the excess. Wrap the orange peel around the inside of the glass. In a mixing glass, combine the tequila, Carpano Antica Formula and bitters; fill with ice and stir well. Strain into the prepared rocks glass. —*François Vera*

GOIABARDENTE

ALLOW 1 DAY FOR INFUSING

Vera reinvents the classic Tommy's Margarita (created in the 1980s at Tommy's Mexican restaurant in San Francisco) with subtly spicy jalapeño-infused agave nectar.

1½ ounces añejo tequila, preferably Ocho
¾ ounce guava nectar
½ ounce fresh lime juice
½ ounce Jalapeño Nectar (below)
Ice, plus 1 large ice cube (page 20) for serving
1 small jalapeño slice, for garnish

In a cocktail shaker, combine the tequila, guava nectar, lime juice and Jalapeño Nectar. Fill the shaker with ice and shake well. Strain into a chilled rocks glass over the large ice cube and place the jalapeño slice on the ice. —*FV*

JALAPEÑO NECTAR

In a jar, combine 5 ounces agave nectar with 2 halved and seeded jalapeños. Cover and refrigerate for 24 hours. Strain into a clean jar, cover and refrigerate for up to 2 weeks. Makes 5 ounces.

GOIABARDENTE

"Newport" glass by Theresienthal from TableArt; "Loggia" wallpaper by Osborne & Little.

PAB'S BUCK

MAKES 8 SERVINGS

ALLOW 2 HOURS FOR CHILLING

This sweet-tart straw-berry cocktail is Vera's homage to his grand-father Pablo Vera, who owned a bar in São Paulo. "He had many regulars who would order the Pablo's Special, a simple blend of berries, sugar, lime and a spirit of their choice," Vera says. "I was only 12 years old at that time, and yes, I had the opportunity to try it once or twice."

8 ounces strawberries, plus 8 strawberries wrapped in lime peels for garnish

⅓ cup superfine sugar

16 ounces añejo tequila

4 ounces triple sec, preferably Combier

4 ounces fresh lime juice

2¼ teaspoons rhubarb bitters

2 tablespoons apple drinking vinegar, such as Bragg

Generous pinch of kosher salt

Ice

16 ounces chilled club soda

In a blender, puree the strawberries and sugar. Blend in all of the remaining ingredients except ice, the soda and garnishes. Refrigerate until chilled, about 2 hours. Strain into a pitcher, stir, then pour the drink into ice-filled collins glasses. Stir in 2 ounces of soda for each and garnish. —*François Vera*

BLACK DAHLIA

The Black Dahlia, created by Leo Robitschek of The NoMad Hotel and Eleven Madison Park in New York City, is an exception to the bartending rule that drinks with citrus juice must be shaken to mix them thoroughly. The small amount of lemon juice here adds brightness and acidity; stirring pre-serves the smoothness of the ingredients.

1 ounce mezcal

¾ ounce Moscatel sherry

½ ounce Grand Marnier

½ ounce Zwack (spicy, herbal Hungarian liqueur)

¾ teaspoon fresh lemon juice

Ice

1 grapefruit twist, for garnish

In a mixing glass, combine all of the ingredients except ice and the garnish; fill with ice and stir well. Strain into a chilled coupe and garnish. —*Leo Robitschek*

PAB'S BUCK
"Stroom" glass by Sugahara from Dandelion; "Kingsburgh" cocktail shaker by Ralph Lauren.

PARIS IS BURNING

Robitschek was inspired to make this smoky-floral cocktail by some smoked pineapples he had during a pig roast in the Hamptons. Mezcal (the agave-based spirit that comes from roasting agave hearts in pits) provides the smokiness.

1 ounce mezcal
1 ounce London dry gin
½ ounce St-Germain elderflower liqueur
1 ounce chilled pineapple juice
½ ounce fresh lemon juice
¼ ounce cane syrup (see Note on page 94)
Ice
Dash of Angostura bitters, for garnish

In a cocktail shaker, combine all of the ingredients except ice and the garnish. Fill the shaker with ice and shake well. Strain into a chilled coupe and garnish with the bitters.
—Leo Robitschek

GRAPES OF WRATH *

Robitschek ingeniously muddles Concord grapes with simple syrup to release their sweet, tangy, fragrant pulp. He pours the muddled grapes over a swizzle of mezcal, sherry and Barolo Chinato, a spiced fortified red wine that enhances the drink's grapey flavor.

*For a mocktail variation, see **P.162**.*

1 ounce mezcal
¾ ounce fino sherry
¾ ounce Barolo Chinato
¾ ounce fresh lemon juice
½ ounce Vanilla Simple Syrup (page 22)
Crushed ice
15 Concord grapes
¼ ounce Simple Syrup (page 22)

In a chilled highball glass, combine the mezcal, sherry, Barolo Chinato, lemon juice and Vanilla Simple Syrup. Fill the glass with crushed ice and mix by spinning a swizzle stick or bar spoon between your hands. In a mixing glass, muddle the grapes with the Simple Syrup and pour over the drink. —LR

CAPRESE DAIQUIRI **P.91**

"Omega" Champagne glasses by Rogaska.

RUM

DRINKS BY:

MATHIAS SIMONIS • THE BON VIVANTS CONSULTING • SAN FRANCISCO

PAUL MCGEE • THREE DOTS & A DASH AND BUB CITY • CHICAGO

JON SANTER • PRIZEFIGHTER • EMERYVILLE, CALIFORNIA

SEAN KENYON • WILLIAMS & GRAHAM • DENVER

GABRIEL ORTA & ELAD ZVI • THE BROKEN SHAKER • MIAMI BEACH

HALLO GOVNA

San Francisco mixologist Mathias Simonis mixes this elegant cocktail with white rum, also known as silver or light rum. He adds berry flavor with a home-made grenadine that has a secret ingredient: raspberry lambic beer.

2 ounces white rum, such as Banks
½ ounce dry orange curaçao, such as Pierre Ferrand
½ ounce dry vermouth
¼ ounce Lambic Grenadine (below)
3 drops of cherry bitters
Ice
1 orange twist, flamed (page 20), for garnish

In a mixing glass, combine all of the ingredients except ice and the garnish. Fill the glass with ice and stir well. Strain into a chilled coupe and garnish with the flamed orange twist. —*Mathias Simonis*

LAMBIC GRENADINE

In a medium saucepan, combine 8 ounces framboise (raspberry) lambic beer with ½ cup sugar and zests from ½ orange and ½ lemon. Bring to a boil, remove from the heat and let cool. Strain the grenadine into a jar and refrigerate for up to 1 month. Makes about 8 ounces.

HALLO GOVNA

ⓄN8ZILLA*

MAKES 10 SERVINGS

ALLOW FOR OVERNIGHT
STEEPING AND 2
HOURS OF CHILLING

This tropical fruit punch is a fantastic make-ahead drink for parties. Simonis named it after the Twitter handle of his friend Nate, who works at Great Lakes Distillery in Milwaukee, Simonis's hometown. Great Lakes makes all kinds of spirits, including the rum and gin that Simonis likes to use in this drink.

*For a mocktail variation, see **P.168**.*

15 ounces white rum

5 ounces gin

5 ounces Galliano (Italian herbal liqueur)

20 ounces fresh orange juice

10 ounces Spiced Pineapple Syrup (below)

1 scant ounce chocolate bitters

1 big block of ice (page 20),
   plus crushed ice for serving

10 pineapple wedges and 10 maraschino cherries,
   for garnish

In a punch bowl, combine all of the ingredients except the ice and garnishes. Refrigerate until chilled, about 2 hours. Stir the punch, then add the big block of ice. Ladle into chilled crushed-ice-filled tiki mugs and garnish each drink with 1 pineapple wedge and 1 cherry.
—*Mathias Simonis*

SPICED PINEAPPLE SYRUP

In a small saucepan, combine 8 ounces unsweetened pineapple juice, ½ cup sugar, 1 teaspoon each of whole cloves, allspice and black peppercorns and 1 split vanilla bean. Bring to a boil, then let cool, cover and steep overnight. Strain the syrup into a jar, cover and refrigerate for up to 2 weeks. Makes about 10 ounces.

PICK 6

Green Bay Packers defensive back and safety Charles Woodson loves this rum-and-Cognac cocktail, which Simonis often made for him at Distil in Milwaukee. The cinnamon syrup makes it ideal for a holiday drink.

1¾ ounces white rum, preferably Puerto Rican
½ ounce Cognac
1 ounce fresh lemon juice
½ ounce cinnamon syrup
3 dashes of orange bitters
Ice, plus 1 large ice cube (page 20) for serving
1 lemon twist, for garnish

In a cocktail shaker, combine the rum, Cognac, lemon juice, cinnamon syrup and bitters. Fill the shaker with ice and shake well. Strain into a chilled rocks glass over the large ice cube and garnish with the lemon twist. —MS

CAPRESE DAIQUIRI

📷 PAGE 87

This ultra-savory daiquiri evokes the flavors of a caprese salad (tomato, basil and fresh mozzarella), one of Simonis's favorite things to eat. He has created versions with oregano-infused rum and extra garnishes like olives and pickled peppers, which are fun to snack on.

4 cherry tomatoes
2 basil leaves
¾ teaspoon balsamic vinegar
Pinch each of salt and freshly ground pepper
2 ounces white rum
¾ ounce Simple Syrup (page 22)
¾ ounce fresh lime juice
Ice
Herbed olive oil and 1 mini mozzarella ball skewered
    with 1 cherry tomato and 1 basil leaf, for garnish

In a cocktail shaker, muddle the 4 cherry tomatoes with the 2 basil leaves, the vinegar, salt and pepper. Add the rum, Simple Syrup and lime juice, fill the shaker with ice and shake well. Fine-strain (**P.21**) into a chilled coupe and garnish with the olive oil, mozzarella ball, cherry tomato and basil leaf. —MS

SANTURCE SPECIAL

Chicago mixologist Paul McGee uses an aged Puerto Rican rum here, which gets depth and character from the time spent in the barrel—a minimum of three years.

2 ounces aged rum, such as
   Ron del Barrilito 2-Star
½ ounce Heering cherry liqueur
½ ounce amontillado sherry
¾ ounce fresh lemon juice
½ ounce Simple Syrup (page 22)
Dash of Angostura bitters
Ice
1 maraschino cherry, preferably Luxardo,
   for garnish

In a cocktail shaker, combine all of the ingredients except ice and the garnish. Fill the shaker with ice and shake well. Fine-strain (**P.21**) into a chilled coupe and garnish with the cherry. —*Paul McGee*

FORGET THE WINTER

For this bright and refreshing drink, McGee mixes in ruby port for its rich, dark-fruit flavors; two kinds of rum; and both Peychaud's and Angostura bitters for balance.

1 ounce Trinidadian rum
¾ ounce ruby port
½ ounce Jamaican rum
¾ ounce fresh lime juice
¾ ounce Simple Syrup (see page 22)
¼ ounce Peychaud's bitters
¼ ounce Angostura bitters
Ice

In a cocktail shaker, combine all of the ingredients except ice. Fill the shaker with ice and shake well. Strain into a chilled ice-filled collins glass. —*PM*

FORGET THE WINTER

"Samira" glass by Theresienthal from TableArt; swizzle stick by Mystic Prism Studio.

TROPIC OF THISTLE

This icy, fresh-mint cocktail is made with amber rum (a.k.a. gold rum). It is usually aged in oak barrels for at least three years, developing caramel and vanilla flavors.

2 ounces blended amber rum, such as
   Banks 7 Golden Age
½ ounce Cynar (bitter artichoke aperitif)
½ ounce Luxardo Amaro Abano
¾ ounce fresh lime juice
½ ounce cane syrup (see Note)
6 large mint leaves
Crushed ice
1 mint sprig, for garnish

In a chilled pilsner glass, combine all of the ingredients except ice and the garnish; fill with crushed ice and mix by spinning a swizzle stick or bar spoon between your hands. Add more crushed ice; garnish with the sprig. —*Paul McGee*
NOTE Cane syrup (concentrated sugarcane juice) is available at Whole Foods and *cocktailkingdom.com*.

RUM RIVER MYSTIC

In Haiti, voodoo priests and priestesses soak the ground with the highest-quality golden Barbancourt rum; they believe it will summon the spirits of the dead. McGee combines it with Trinidadian rum in this drink.

1 ounce amber Haitian rum
1 ounce Trinidadian rum
¾ ounce Byrrh Grand Quinquina
   (slightly bitter aperitif wine)
¼ ounce Bénédictine (spiced herbal liqueur)
2 dashes of Angostura bitters
Ice, plus 1 large ice cube (page 20) for serving
1 orange twist, for garnish

In a mixing glass, combine all of the ingredients except ice and the garnish; fill with ice and stir well. Pour into a chilled double rocks glass over the large ice cube and garnish with the orange twist. —*PM*

JEFFERSON SOUR

"I wanted to make a sour the oldest way possible, with sugar, not simple syrup," says California mixologist Jon Santer, "then put a spin on it with an old-fashioned ingredient like ruby port—port being a founding wine of this country." (It was a staple in Thomas Jefferson's wine cellar.)

1½ teaspoons superfine sugar
¾ ounce fresh lemon juice
2 ounces aged rum,
  preferably Dos Maderas P.X. 5 + 5
Ice
¾ ounce ruby port

In a cocktail shaker, stir the sugar and lemon juice until the sugar dissolves. Add the rum, fill the shaker with ice and shake well. Strain into a chilled ice-filled double rocks glass and top with the ruby port. —*Jon Santer*

HARDWOOD

"I'm in love with sherry of all types as a cocktail ingredient," Santer says. "I know I'm late to this party, but I'm just trying to contribute!" Here he uses cream sherry and gives the drink a double dose of cloves with Velvet Falernum liqueur and Jerry Thomas' Own Decanter bitters (the-bitter-truth.com).

1½ ounces aged rum, preferably Venezuelan
½ ounce cream sherry
¼ ounce Velvet Falernum (clove-spiced liqueur)
2 dashes of The Bitter Truth
  Jerry Thomas' Own Decanter bitters
Ice
1 lemon twist, for garnish

In a mixing glass, combine the rum, sherry, Velvet Falernum and bitters; fill the glass with ice and stir well. Strain into a chilled coupe and garnish with the lemon twist. —*JS*

MEDFORD WARMER

Now a resident of Northern California, Santer grew up near Medford, Massachusetts, which once produced much of the rum in the United States. "When I think about rum drinks I think about New England fall flavors like apples and mulling spices," he says about this hot toddy.

1 clove-studded lemon wheel
2 ounces aged Trinidadian rum, preferably Angostura 1919
½ ounce dark crème de cacao, preferably Tempus Fugit
4½ ounces hot water
¾ ounce Apple Juice Reduction (below)
Dash of Angostura bitters

Place the clove-studded lemon wheel in a heatproof glass. Add the rum, dark crème de cacao, hot water, Apple Juice Reduction and bitters and stir well. —*Jon Santer*

APPLE JUICE REDUCTION
In a small saucepan, simmer 2 cups unfiltered apple juice over moderate heat until reduced to ½ cup. Let cool. Pour into a jar and refrigerate for up to 2 weeks. Makes 4 ounces.

NORCAL FLIP

"This is such a California-cuisine drink, even I'm rolling my eyes," Santer says about his sweet and salty flip (a spirit mixed with a whole egg, sugar and spice). He recomments using an artisanal almond-flavored syrup like Small Hand Foods orgeat or making your own. "Don't buy the fake stuff," he implores.

2 ounces aged Guyanese rum, preferably El Dorado 12
¾ ounce orgeat
1 large egg
1 teaspoon extra-virgin olive oil
Ice
Pinch of sea salt, for garnish

In a cocktail shaker, combine the rum, orgeat, egg and oil and shake vigorously. Fill the shaker with ice and shake again. Fine-strain (**P.21**) into a chilled coupe and garnish with the salt. —*JS*

MEDFORD WARMER
Murano glass bowl from The End of History.

THE TEMPEST

This riff on a Dark and Stormy is from Sean Kenyon, the owner and barkeep of Williams & Graham in Denver. "With a hurricane of spices in the rum as well as ginger and Angostura bitters, it may seem too much," he says, "but the peaches tie it all together."

⅛ medium peach, plus 1 peach slice for garnish
½ ounce fresh lemon juice
2 dashes of Angostura bitters
1½ ounces spiced rum
Ice
3 ounces chilled ginger beer

In a cocktail shaker, muddle the peach wedge with the lemon juice and bitters. Add the rum, then fill the shaker with ice and shake well. Strain into a chilled ice-filled collins or highball glass, stir in the ginger beer and garnish with the peach slice. —*Sean Kenyon*

SAILING ON *

Kenyon recommends making this cocktail with nutmeg-and-allspice-inflected Chairman's Reserve spiced rum. Honey steeped with dried habanero gives the drink a persistent warmth. "On the first sip it seems only slightly spicy, but it builds," he says. "It's amazing how the cocktail evolves as you drink it."

For a mocktail variation, see **P.164.*

1½ ounces spiced rum
½ ounce apricot liqueur
½ ounce fresh lemon juice
¼ ounce Honey-Habanero Syrup
   (page 164)
Ice
1 lemon twist, for garnish

In a cocktail shaker, combine the rum, apricot liqueur, lemon juice and Honey-Habanero Syrup. Fill the shaker with ice and shake well. Strain into a chilled coupe, then pinch the lemon twist over the drink and drop it in. —*SK*

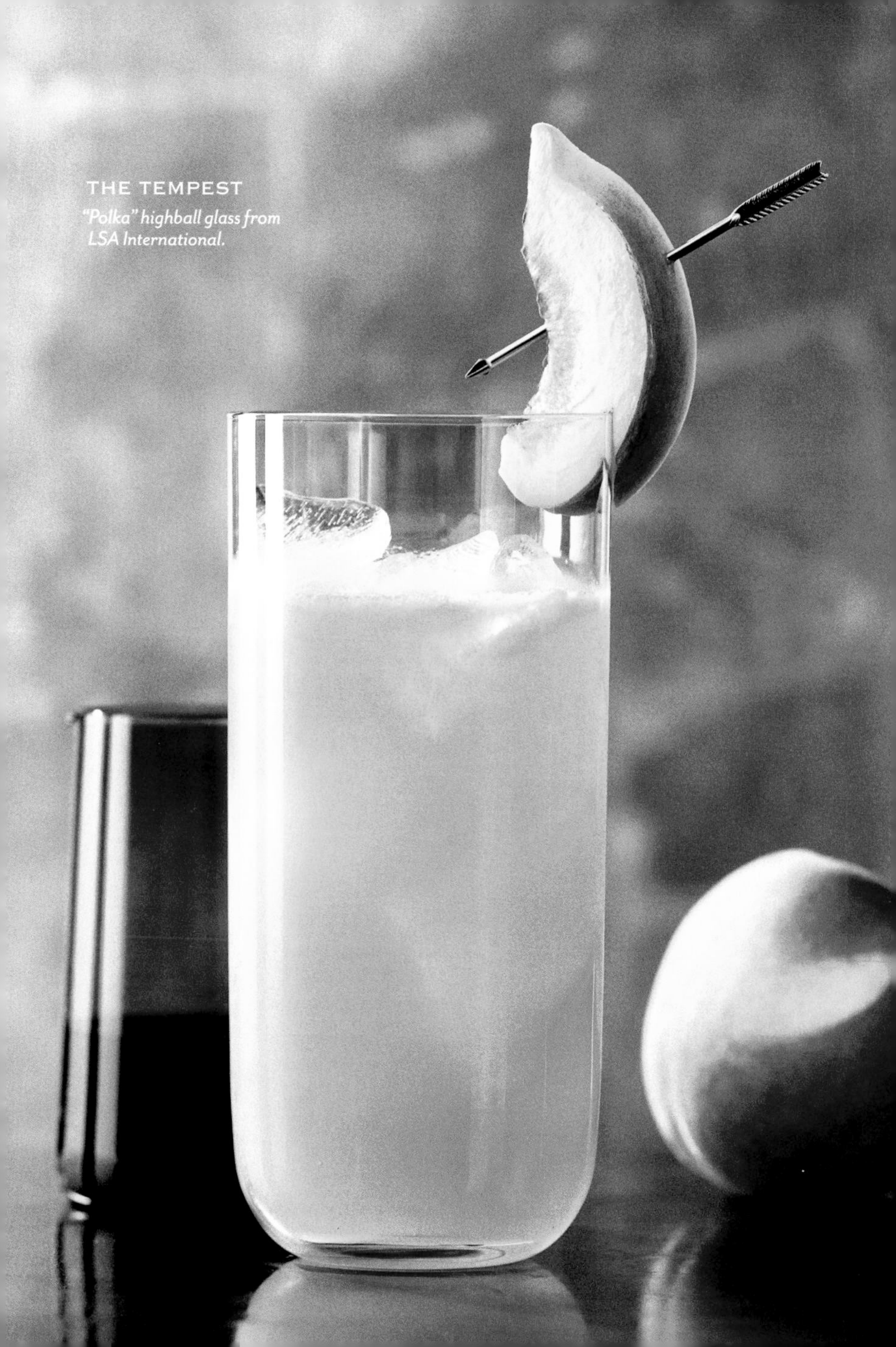

THE TEMPEST

"Polka" highball glass from LSA International.

Rum

RUFFIAN SPORTING CLUB PUNCH

MAKES ABOUT 8 SERVINGS

ALLOW 6 DAYS FOR STEEPING AND 2 HOURS FOR CHILLING

For this punch, Kenyon creates his own spiced rum, infusing it with cinnamon, ginger, vanilla and orange zest. As an unexpected twist, he adds Earl Grey tea for a chai-like flavor.

RUFFIAN SPICED RUM

One 2-inch piece of cinnamon stick
2 allspice berries
4 pink peppercorns
2 pinches of ground cloves
16 ounces aged Nicaraguan rum, preferably 7-year-old
1½ teaspoons ground ginger
1 teaspoon finely grated orange zest
½ Madagascar vanilla bean, split
½ ounce Rich Simple Syrup (page 22)

PUNCH

8 ounces Cognac, preferably Pierre Ferrand 1840
4 ounces fortified Muscat aperitif wine, preferably Barsol Perfecto Amor Moscato
16 ounces chilled strong-brewed Earl Grey tea
8 ounces fresh lemon juice
8 ounces Rich Simple Syrup (page 22)
Ice

1. In a spice grinder, combine the cinnamon stick, allspice, peppercorns and ground cloves and coarsely grind.
2. In a small skillet, toast the spices over medium-high heat until fragrant, about 6 minutes. Transfer to a large jar and stir in the rum, ground ginger, orange zest, vanilla and ½ ounce Rich Simple Syrup. Cover and let stand at room temperature for 6 days; shake the jar once a day.
3. Strain the rum into a punch bowl. Stir in the remaining ingredients except ice. Refrigerate until chilled, 2 hours.
4. To serve, fill a shaker with ice. Working in batches, stir the punch, ladle into the shaker and shake well. Strain into chilled rocks glasses. —*Sean Kenyon*

OLD IRONSIDES

*"Many people treat rum like it's only for summer,"
Kenyon says. "I wanted
to create a cold-weather
rum drink." He uses
Sailor Jerry spiced Navy
rum, which has a higher
proof than most rums and
hints of cherry, cinnamon
and cloves.*

2 ounces spiced rum
½ ounce Heering cherry liqueur
½ ounce Cynar (bitter artichoke aperitif)
Ice, plus 1 large ice cube (page 20) for serving
1 maraschino cherry, for garnish

In a mixing glass, combine the rum, Heering and Cynar;
fill with ice and stir well. Strain into a chilled rocks glass
over the large ice cube and garnish with the cherry. —SK

SWEET MARY SWIZZLE *

*Miami mixologists
Gabriel Orta and Elad
Zvi love using soursop
juice in cocktails. It has a
slightly tart, tropical
creaminess that's fantas-
tic with rhum agri-
cole (an aromatic French
West Indian rum made
from sugarcane juice).
"Add some pineapple juice
and a touch of sweet-
spicy liqueur and you have
a great island party,"
Orta says.*

**For a mocktail variation,
see **P.168**.*

2 ounces rhum agricole, preferably amber,
   such as Élevé Sous Bois
¾ ounce Velvet Falernum (clove-spiced liqueur)
1 ounce chilled soursop juice (available at
   Latin markets and *amazon.com*)
½ ounce fresh lemon juice
¼ ounce chilled unsweetened pineapple juice
Ice cubes, plus crushed ice for serving
2 dashes of Peychaud's bitters
1 mint sprig, for garnish

In a cocktail shaker, combine the rum, Velvet Falernum
and 3 juices. Fill the shaker with ice cubes and shake well.
Strain into a chilled crushed-ice-filled collins glass, swizzle briefly, then top with the bitters and garnish with the
mint sprig. —Gabriel Orta and Elad Zvi

RHUM & FUNK

**ALLOW 3 HOURS
FOR STEEPING**

The rhum agricole in this drink is infused with a delicious but unusual ingredient: Cocoa Puffs cereal. "People go crazy for it when we serve it," Zvi says. "It sounds insane, but the flavors work."

1 sugar cube

2 dashes of orange bitters

Dash of Angostura bitters

2½ ounces Cocoa Puffs Rhum (below)

Ice

1 spiral-cut orange twist (page 20), for garnish

In a chilled rocks glass, muddle the sugar with both bitters and the Cocoa Puffs Rhum; fill with ice and and stir well. Garnish with the twist. —*Gabriel Orta and Elad Zvi*

COCOA PUFFS RHUM

In a bowl, combine 1½ cups Cocoa Puffs cereal and 8 ounces aged rhum agricole; let stand at room temperature for 3 hours. Strain into a jar, cover and store at room temperature for up to 1 month. Makes about 8 ounces.

FAVELA BEACH

"You don't see a lot of strong and intense flavors in stirred cachaça cocktails," Orta says. "This is definitely strong, intense and bittersweet." Cachaça (the potent spirit used in the caipirinha) is similar to rum but made from sugarcane juice rather than molasses.

2 ounces aged cachaça

½ ounce Licor 43 (citrus-and-vanilla-flavored Spanish liqueur)

¼ ounce Cocchi Americano (fortified, slightly bitter aperitif wine)

¾ teaspoon Cynar (bitter artichoke aperitif)

2 dashes of orange bitters

Ice

1 orange twist, for garnish

In a mixing glass, combine all of the ingredients except ice and the garnish; fill with ice and stir well. Strain into a chilled coupe and garnish with the twist. —*GO and EZ*

RHUM & FUNK
"Fluent" glass by Moser.

ESSENTIAL

"The Essential is a great balance between citrusy and creamy, with a beautiful aroma of flowers and sugarcane," says Zvi. "In a perfect world, I would like to drink it on some crazy night in Rio de Janeiro." The cocktail is best made with a milder young Brazilian cachaça, one that's aged for no more than six months.

2 ounces cachaça
1 ounce Hibiscus Cordial (below)
¾ ounce fresh lime juice
1 large egg white
Ice
1 fresh hibiscus flower, for garnish (optional)

In a cocktail shaker, combine the cachaça, Hibiscus Cordial, lime juice and egg white and shake vigorously. Fill the shaker with ice and shake again. Strain into a chilled rocks glass (with ice or without) and garnish the drink with the hibiscus flower. —*Gabriel Orta and Elad Zvi*

HIBISCUS CORDIAL

In a small saucepan, boil 4 ounces water. Reduce the heat to medium and add 2 tablespoons hibiscus tea (dried hibiscus flowers, available at Latin markets and health food stores) and ¾ cup sugar, stirring until the sugar dissolves. Remove from the heat and let cool. Stir in ¾ ounce 100 proof vodka, ½ teaspoon port and ¼ teaspoon each of orange blossom water and rose water. Strain the cordial into a jar, cover and refrigerate for up to 1 month. Makes about 8 ounces.

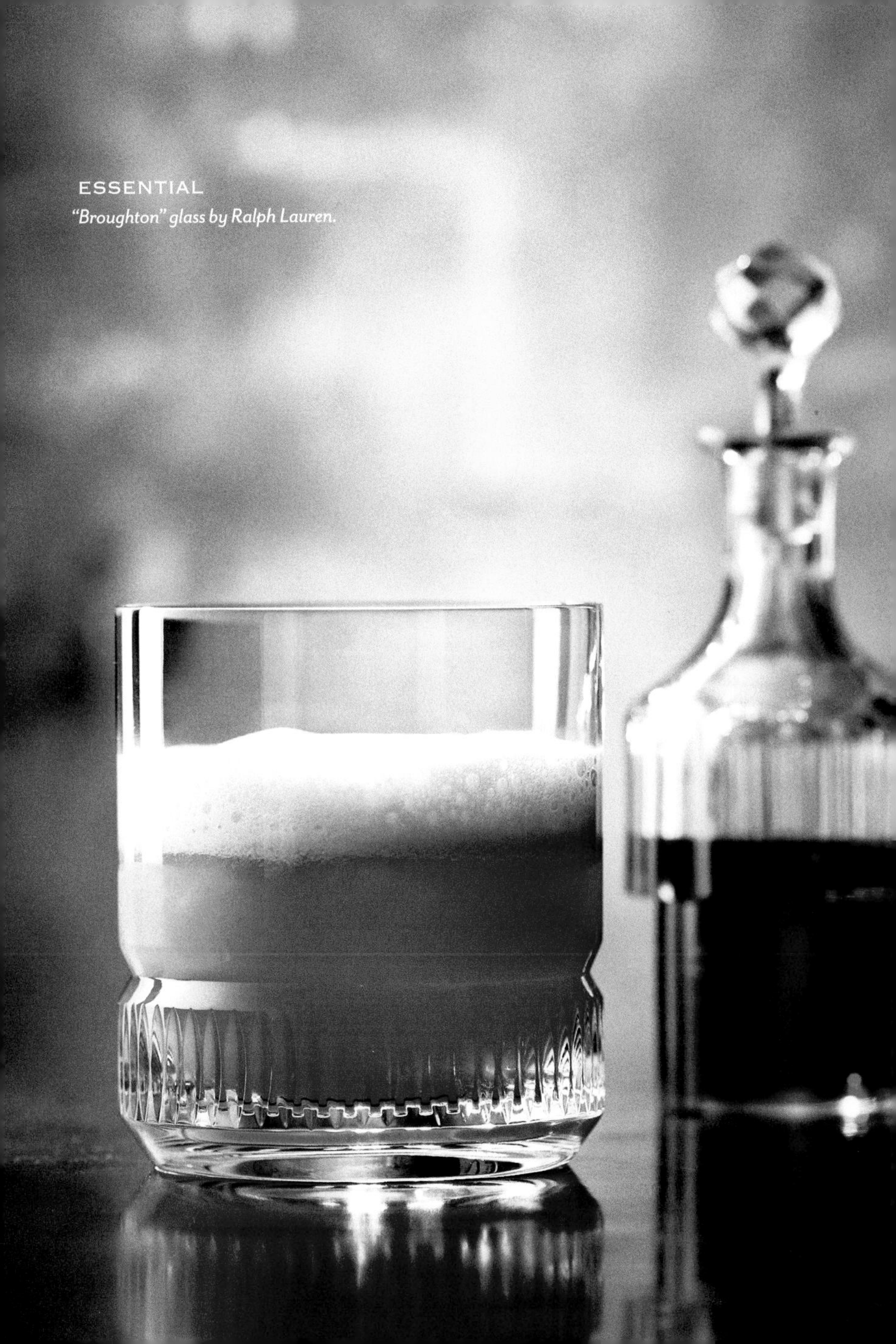

ESSENTIAL

"Broughton" glass by Ralph Lauren.

FOGGY DEW **P.110**
"Sarjaton" glasses by Iittala;
floral bowl by Aerin.

WHISKEY

DRINKS BY:

JACK MCGARRY • THE DEAD RABBIT GROCERY & GROG • NEW YORK CITY

GREG BUTTERA & STEPHEN COLE • THE BARRELHOUSE FLAT • CHICAGO

JOSH DURR • HAWTHORN BEVERAGE CONSULTING • LOUISVILLE

BILL NORRIS • MIDNIGHT COWBOY • AUSTIN

JOHN DEBARY • PDT AND MOMOFUKU • NEW YORK CITY

BANKERS ARE WANKERS

ALLOW 2 HOURS FOR
MACERATING

*Jack McGarry of The
Dead Rabbit Grocery and
Grog in New York City
makes his own easy rasp-
berry cordial to shake
with Irish whiskey (a type
of whiskey that tends to
be lighter and less smoky
than Scotch). He adds
Orinoco bitters, a 19th-
century style of bitters
similar to Angostura. The
Dead Rabbit, which spe-
cializes in cocktails from
the 19th century, bottles
and sells its own bitters at
deadrabbitnyc.com.*

1 ounce Irish whiskey, preferably 12-year-old
1 ounce Jamaican rum
1 ounce late bottled vintage port
1 ounce Raspberry Cordial (below)
¾ ounce fresh lime juice
3 dashes of The Dead Rabbit Orinoco bitters
   or Angostura bitters
Ice
Pinch of freshly grated nutmeg, for garnish

In a cocktail shaker, combine all of the ingredients except
ice and the garnish. Fill the shaker with ice and shake well.
Strain into a chilled ice-filled rocks glass and garnish with
the nutmeg. —*Jack McGarry*

RASPBERRY CORDIAL

In a blender or food processor, puree 3 ounces (about ½
cup) fresh raspberries. Transfer to a medium bowl. Add
¾ cup superfine sugar and 6 ounces cold water and stir
until the sugar dissolves. Let macerate at room temperature for 2 hours. Strain the Raspberry Cordial into a jar
and refrigerate for up to 2 weeks. Makes about 12 ounces.

BANKERS ARE WANKERS

"Mipreshus" glass by Nouvel Studio; "Crocodilo" wallpaper by Osborne & Little.

Whiskey

DUNEDEN

McGarry gives complexity to this riff on the Manhattan with absinthe and the spiced violet liqueur parfait amour. "Seeing as we have all these Manhattan variations named for Brooklyn neighborhoods like Red Hook and Greenpoint knocking about," he says, "I decided to name mine after the very street where I was born in Northern Ireland."

2¼ ounces Irish whiskey, preferably 12-year-old
1 ounce sweet vermouth
½ ounce parfait amour
1 teaspoon absinthe, preferably Pernod
2 dashes of orange bitters
Ice
1 lemon twist

In a mixing glass, combine all of the ingredients except ice and the twist; fill with ice and stir well. Strain into a chilled coupe. Pinch the lemon twist over the drink and discard. —Jack McGarry

FOGGY DEW

📷 PAGE 107

McGarry combines raisiny Pedro Ximénez sherry and vanilla-inflected Jameson Black Barrel whiskey to create this Irish take on eggnog.

1½ ounces Irish whiskey, preferably 12-year-old
1 ounce Jamaican rum
1 ounce Pedro Ximénez sherry
1½ ounces chilled half-and-half
½ ounce Vanilla Simple Syrup (page 22)
1 large egg
Ice
Pinch of freshly grated nutmeg, for garnish

In a cocktail shaker, combine all of the ingredients except ice and the garnish and shake vigorously. Fill the shaker with ice and shake again. Strain into a chilled mug or fizz glass and garnish with the nutmeg. —JM

NANCY WHISKEY

To give this cocktail an intense smokiness, McGarry prefers a peated Irish whiskey (whiskey distilled from malt dried over peat fires—a process used in Scotch production but unusual for Irish whiskey). The honey and ginger syrup help balance the smokiness.

2 ounces Irish whiskey, preferably a peated single malt, such as Connemara

½ ounce Branca Menta (bitter, minty Italian digestif)

¾ ounce fresh lemon juice

½ ounce Ginger Syrup (page 130)

½ ounce honey syrup (2 teaspoons honey mixed with 1 teaspoon warm water)

Ice

1½ ounces chilled club soda

1 lemon twist

Pinch of freshly grated nutmeg, for garnish

In a cocktail shaker, combine the whiskey, Branca Menta, lemon juice, Ginger Syrup and honey syrup. Fill the shaker with ice and shake well. Strain into a chilled ice-filled high-ball glass and stir in the club soda. Pinch the lemon twist over the drink and discard. Garnish with the nutmeg. —JM

CASTING ASPERSIONS

For this citrusy cocktail, Greg Buttera and Stephen Cole of The Barrelhouse Flat in Chicago use MBR Black Dog Kentucky corn whiskey, a clear unaged white whiskey. Some of the corn that goes into Black Dog is "dark-fired" in a tobacco barn, making the whiskey smokier than other white varieties.

2 ounces white whiskey,
   preferably MBR Black Dog Kentucky corn
¾ ounce fresh lemon juice
¾ ounce fresh grapefruit juice
½ ounce honey syrup (2 teaspoons honey
   mixed with 1 teaspoon warm water)
½ ounce Amaro Nonino
   (bittersweet herbal digestif)
Dash of Angostura bitters
Ice
1 mint sprig, for garnish

In a cocktail shaker, combine all of the ingredients except ice and the garnish. Fill the shaker with ice and shake well. Strain into a chilled ice-filled rocks glass and garnish with the mint sprig. —*Greg Buttera and Stephen Cole*

CABIN IN THE WOODS

Buttera and Cole prefer light, smooth Canadian whisky for their Cabin in the Woods. They give the drink depths of orange flavor with orange curaçao, orange bitters and an orange twist that's pinched over the drink to squeeze out the essential oils in the peel.

2 ounces Canadian whisky
¾ ounce ruby port, preferably Warre's Warrior
¼ ounce mezcal
¼ ounce orange curaçao
¾ teaspoon Fernet-Branca (bitter Italian digestif)
Dash of Angostura bitters
Dash of orange bitters
Ice
1 orange twist

In a mixing glass, combine all of the ingredients except ice and the twist; fill with ice and stir well. Strain into a chilled coupe. Pinch the twist over the drink; discard. —*GB and SC*

CASTING ASPERSIONS

"Gigolo" glass by Nason Moretti from TableArt.

LUCHADOR

"I wanted to build up layers of spice in this cocktail," says Buttera. "The effect is a little like Christmas pudding."

1½ ounces white whiskey, preferably corn
½ ounce sweet vermouth, preferably Punt e Mes
½ ounce Cardamaro (spiced, bittersweet herbal digestif)
¼ ounce amontillado sherry, preferably Lustau
Dash of orange bitters
Ice
1 orange twist

In a mixing glass, combine all of the ingredients except ice and the orange twist; fill with ice and stir well. Strain into a chilled coupe. Pinch the twist over the drink and discard. —*Greg Buttera and Stephen Cole*

BARE KNUCKLE

White whiskey is having its moment in the US right now. Since the whiskey isn't aged in barrels, distillers are able to release it quickly. Buttera and Cole mix their Bare Knuckle with High West Silver OMG Pure Rye, made in Park City, Utah.

1½ ounces white whiskey, preferably rye-based
1 ounce Carpano Antica Formula or other sweet vermouth
¼ ounce Cynar (bitter artichoke aperitif)
¼ ounce Fernet-Branca (bitter Italian digestif)
2 dashes of Angostura bitters
2 mint sprigs, lightly bruised
Ice
1 lemon twist

In a mixing glass, combine all of the ingredients except ice and the twist. Fill with ice and stir well, then strain into a chilled coupe. Pinch the twist over the drink and discard. —*GB and SC*

EYES WIDE SHUT

MAKES 8 SERVINGS

ALLOW FOR OVERNIGHT
MACERATING AND
2 HOURS OF CHILLING

Louisville mixology consultant Josh Durr flavors this bourbon-grapefruit drink with a simple syrup made from fresh raspberries. This recipe is ideal for parties because rather than shaking each cocktail individually, you can prepare a big batch in advance.

2 ounces fresh raspberries (about ⅓ cup)

¼ cup plus 2 tablespoons superfine sugar

16 ounces bourbon,
preferably Four Roses Single Barrel

8 ounces fresh grapefruit juice

2 ounces fresh lime juice

32 dashes (about 1 ounce) of Peychaud's bitters

Ice

16 ounces chilled club soda

8 grapefruit twists, for garnish

1. In a blender or food processor, puree the raspberries with the sugar and 4 ounces cold water. Transfer the raspberry syrup to a jar, cover and refrigerate overnight.

2. Strain the syrup into a pitcher, then stir in the bourbon, grapefruit juice, lime juice and bitters. Refrigerate until chilled, about 2 hours.

3. Stir the drink, then pour into 8 chilled ice-filled collins glasses. Stir 2 ounces of club soda into each drink and garnish with the grapefruit twists. —*Josh Durr*

THE MALONEY NO. 2

Durr insists on bonded bourbon (a high-octane version that is at least 50 percent alcohol) for this drink. "You need the higher proof to balance the cocktail," he says. "Lower proofs fall flat on the tongue."

1½ ounces bonded bourbon, such as
    Old Fitzgerald bottled in bond 100 proof
1½ ounces sweet vermouth
¾ ounce Cynar (bitter artichoke aperitif)
¼ ounce maraschino liqueur
Ice
1 orange twist, for garnish

In a mixing glass, combine the bourbon, vermouth, Cynar and maraschino liqueur; fill with ice and stir well. Strain into a chilled ice-filled double rocks glass and garnish with the orange twist. —*Josh Durr*

THE DARK SIDE

All bourbons combine corn and other grains. Durr prefers this cocktail with a high-rye bourbon (one made with more rye), creating a bolder and spicier flavor.

2 ounces bourbon, preferably high-rye,
    such as Bulleit
1 ounce Bonal Gentiane-Quina
    (slightly bitter aperitif wine)
¾ ounce fresh lime juice
¾ ounce Simple Syrup (page 22)
2 dashes of orange bitters
Ice
1 ounce chilled club soda
1 mint sprig, for garnish

In a cocktail shaker, combine the bourbon, Bonal, lime juice, Simple Syrup and bitters. Fill the shaker with ice and shake well. Fine-strain (**P.21**) into a chilled ice-filled collins or highball glass, stir in the club soda and garnish with the mint sprig. —*JD*

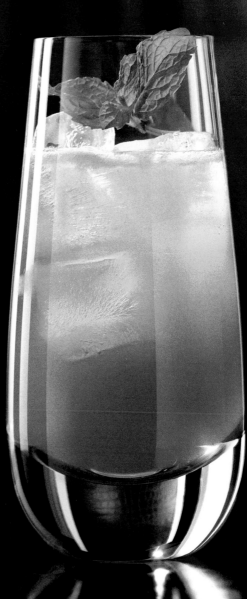

THE DARK SIDE

*"Yola" highball glass from
LSA International.*

LUMBERJACK JULEP

Playing on the classic bourbon-based mint julep, Durr adds rye whiskey and replaces the conventional simple syrup with maple syrup.

4 mint sprigs
1 ounce bourbon, preferably port-barrel-finished
1 ounce bonded rye whiskey, preferably Rittenhouse Rye 100 proof
¼ ounce pure maple syrup
Crushed ice

In a chilled julep cup, muddle 3 of the mint sprigs. Add the bourbon, rye and maple syrup; fill the cup with crushed ice and mix the drink by spinning a swizzle stick or bar spoon between your hands. Top with more crushed ice and garnish with the remaining mint sprig. Serve with a cut straw. —*Josh Durr*

PLUM TUCKERED

Bill Norris of Austin's Midnight Cowboy mixes this drink with rye whiskey and Gekkeikan Kobai plum wine from California. The wine is made by steeping plums in white wine instead of the typical Japanese shochu (a low-proof vodka-like spirit).

1½ ounces rye whiskey
1½ ounces plum wine
½ ounce Campari
Cracked ice, plus ice cubes for serving
1 spiral-cut orange twist (page 20), for garnish

In a mixing glass, combine the rye, plum wine and Campari; fill with cracked ice and stir well. Strain into a chilled ice-cube-filled rocks glass and garnish with the orange twist. —*Bill Norris*

THE ROUND TABLE

Rather than blending orange bitters into the drink, Norris uses them as a fragrant garnish. You can add the bitters as drops, as Norris does, or mist them over the drink with an atomizer (available at beauty-supply stores and muji.us).

2 ounces bonded rye whiskey, preferably Rittenhouse Rye 100 proof

½ ounce sake, such as Gekkeikan

1 ounce chilled unsweetened pineapple juice

¾ ounce honey syrup (1 tablespoon honey mixed with ½ tablespoon warm water)

1 large egg white

Ice

2 drops of orange bitters, for garnish

In a cocktail shaker, combine all of the ingredients except ice and the bitters and shake vigorously. Fill the shaker with ice and shake again. Strain into a chilled white wine glass and garnish with the bitters. —*BN*

FULL SCOTCH-IRISH BREAKFAST

Maple syrup, lemon curd and a whole egg are shaken with rye whiskey and stout beer in the Full Scotch-Irish Breakfast. It's Norris's tribute to the Scotch-Irish pioneers who were the first to distill whiskey in America.

2 ounces rye whiskey, preferably Bulleit

1 ounce stout beer, such as Guinness

½ ounce pure maple syrup

2 teaspoons lemon curd

2 dashes of mole bitters

1 large egg

Ice

Small pinch of freshly grated nutmeg, for garnish

In a cocktail shaker, combine all of the ingredients except ice and the garnish and shake vigorously. Fill the shaker with ice and shake again. Strain into a chilled coupe and garnish with the nutmeg. —*BN*

THE TURKEY'S WATTLE

Inspired by a punch that Norris made for Thanksgiving one year, the Turkey's Wattle gets its wonderful autumnal flavor from apple cider, ginger beer and a bit of allspice liqueur.

2½ ounces rye whiskey, preferably Wild Turkey Rye 101 proof

¾ teaspoon St. Elizabeth allspice dram (rum-based allspice liqueur)

1 ounce chilled apple cider

½ ounce Simple Syrup (page 22)

Two 6-inch strips of orange zest

Ice

2 ounces chilled ginger beer

In a cocktail shaker, combine the whiskey, allspice dram, cider, Simple Syrup and 1 of the orange zest strips. Fill the shaker with ice and shake well, then strain into a chilled ice-filled collins glass. Stir in the ginger beer and garnish with the remaining strip of orange zest. —*Bill Norris*

KANSAI KICK

New York City mixologist John deBary, who tested all of the drinks for this book, created this variation on Cameron's Kick (Scotch, Irish whiskey, orgeat and lemon juice). An enthusiast of all things Japanese—he lived near the Suntory Yamazaki distillery when he was working in Japan—deBary uses Japanese whisky, which is similar in style to Scotch.

1½ ounces Japanese whisky, preferably Yamazaki 12-year-old

¾ ounce Sercial Madeira

¾ ounce fresh lime juice

Scant ½ ounce orgeat (almond-flavored syrup)

Ice

In a cocktail shaker, combine the whisky, Madeira, lime juice and orgeat. Fill the shaker with ice and shake well. Strain into a chilled coupe. —*John deBary*

KANSAI KICK

"Yukiwa" shaker from Cocktail Kingdom.

NORTHERN HEMISPHERE

MAKES 8 SERVINGS

Spirits from northern islands (Bermuda, Scotland's Islay and Japan) form the basis of this tiki drink that boasts grilled pineapple juice. "Curaçao, grenadine and, of course, the umbrella supply the tiki cred," says deBary.

Seven ½-inch-thick pineapple wheels—2 unpeeled and 5 peeled
About ¼ cup pineapple juice
6 ounces Japanese whisky
6 ounces Islay Scotch
6 ounces dark rum, preferably Gosling's Black Seal
4 ounces orange curaçao
4 ounces fresh orange juice
4 ounces fresh lemon juice
4 ounces grenadine, preferably homemade (page 22)
Ice
8 small hollowed pineapples, for serving (optional)
8 cocktail umbrellas, for garnish

1. Preheat a grill pan over high heat. Grill all of the pineapple wheels until they are charred, about 5 minutes per side. Cut each unpeeled pineapple wheel into 4 wedges and reserve them for garnish.

2. Cut the peeled pineapple wheels into small pieces. In a blender, puree the peeled pieces, adding up to ¼ cup pineapple juice to help blend. Strain the puree into a measuring cup, transfer 8 ounces of the grilled pineapple juice to a pitcher (reserve the rest for another use), then stir in the whisky, Scotch, rum, curaçao, orange juice, lemon juice and grenadine.

3. Pour half of the mixture into the blender, add 2 cups of ice and blend until slushy. Pour into 8 chilled tiki mugs or hollowed pineapples. Garnish each drink with a grilled pineapple wedge and a cocktail umbrella. Repeat for the remaining servings. —*John deBary*

HIGHLAND TODDY *

"Licorice tea is one of my favorite nonalcoholic beverages," deBary says. "So why not do what any sensible person would do and add alcohol?" Accordingly, he blends the hot, soothing tea with Scotch and ginger liqueur.

*For a mocktail variation, see **P.162.**

1 ounce Highland Scotch
½ ounce ginger liqueur
6 ounces hot brewed licorice tea
¾ teaspoon honey syrup (½ teaspoon honey mixed with ¼ teaspoon warm water)
1 lemon wedge, for garnish

In a warmed mug or heatproof glass, combine all of the ingredients except the garnish and stir well. Squeeze the lemon wedge over the drink and drop it in. —JD

DOUBLE-BARRELED MARTINEZ

DeBary reimagines the classic Martinez (gin, vermouth, maraschino liqueur and orange bitters) with Balvenie Double-Wood single malt. The Scotch gets a distinctive flavor from aging in two kinds of wood—first in traditional whisky barrels, then in sherry casks.

1 ounce single-malt Scotch
¾ ounce Lustau East India Solera sherry
¼ ounce maraschino liqueur
2 dashes of orange bitters
Ice
1 orange twist, for garnish

In a mixing glass, combine the Scotch, sherry, maraschino liqueur and bitters; fill with ice and stir well. Strain into a chilled coupe and garnish with the orange twist. —JD

BRANDY

DRINKS BY:

TOMMY KLUS • MULTNOMAH WHISKEY LIBRARY • PORTLAND, OREGON

CHRIS HANNAH • ARNAUD'S FRENCH 75 BAR • NEW ORLEANS

NICOLE LEBEDEVITCH • THE HAWTHORNE • BOSTON

LINDSAY NADER • ELYSIUM CRAFT COCKTAIL SERVICES • LOS ANGELES

BEHIND THE FAÇADE
P.137

"Chandi" glasses by Paola Navone
for Egizia from TableArt.

FORTUNATE PLUM

Tommy Klus, a mixologist based in Portland, Oregon, combines two types of brandy for this drink: the South American grape-based pisco and Clear Creek plum brandy, a domestic brandy made with Oregon blue plums.

1 ounce plum brandy
1 ounce pisco, preferably Chilean
¾ ounce Cocchi Americano
  (fortified, slightly bitter aperitif wine)
¼ ounce yellow Chartreuse (spicy herbal liqueur)
Ice
1 lemon twist
1 thyme sprig, for garnish

In a mixing glass, combine the plum brandy, pisco, Cocchi Americano and Chartreuse; fill with ice and stir well, then strain into a chilled coupe. Pinch the lemon twist over the drink and discard. Garnish with the thyme sprig.
—*Tommy Klus*

SENDERO TRAIL

Bright, floral and tart, the Sendero Trail is Klus's alternative to the classic pisco sour. First he shakes the ingredients without ice (a.k.a. dry-shaking) to emulsify the egg white and give the drink an airy texture. He then shakes the cocktail again with ice to chill it.

1 ounce plum brandy
1 ounce pisco, preferably Chilean
½ ounce triple sec, preferably Combier
¾ ounce fresh lime juice
¾ ounce passion fruit syrup
1 large egg white, lightly beaten
Ice
3 drops of Angostura bitters, for garnish

In a cocktail shaker, combine the plum brandy, pisco, triple sec, lime juice, passion fruit syrup and egg white and shake vigorously. Fill the shaker with ice and shake again. Fine-strain (**P.21**) into a chilled coupe and dot the bitters across the top of the drink. —*TK*

FORTUNATE PLUM

"Excess" pitcher by Saint-Louis.

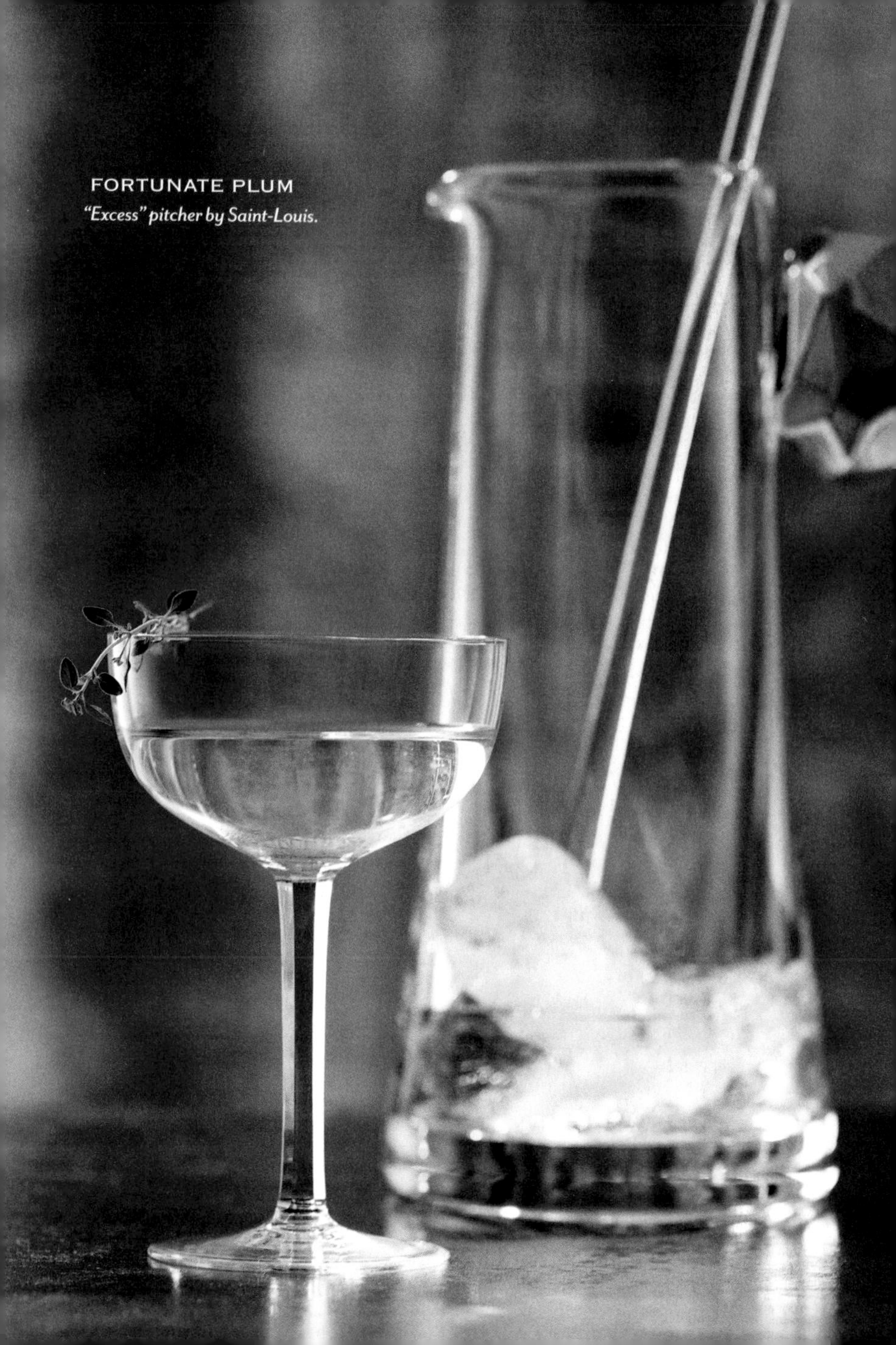

WICKED GAMES

Klus conceived of this pineapple-and-ginger-flavored drink while having lunch at Fish Sauce, a modern Vietnamese restaurant in Portland. "The owner, Ben Bui, kindly allowed me to jump behind the bar and bring this vacation-inspired cocktail to life," he says.

1¼ ounces pear brandy
¾ ounce mezcal
¾ ounce fresh lemon juice
¾ ounce chilled unsweetened pineapple juice
½ ounce Ginger Syrup (below)
Ice cubes, plus crushed ice for serving
1 thin slice of fresh ginger and 2 pineapple leaves (optional), for garnish

In a cocktail shaker, combine the brandy, mezcal, lemon juice, pineapple juice and Ginger Syrup. Fill the shaker with ice cubes and shake well. Strain the drink into a chilled crushed-ice-filled collins glass and garnish with the ginger slice and pineapple leaves. —*Tommy Klus*

GINGER SYRUP

In a small saucepan, combine ½ cup sugar with 4 ounces water. Simmer over moderate heat, stirring, until the sugar dissolves. Add ⅓ cup minced fresh ginger and simmer over low heat for 30 minutes, stirring occasionally. Let cool, then pour the syrup through a fine strainer into a jar. Refrigerate for up to 2 weeks. Makes about 5 ounces.

WICKED GAMES

PROSPECTOR

Klus's original version of the Prospector included honey syrup infused with pipe tobacco. "After customers suddenly became addicted, I decided to drop the tobacco," he says. "But the cocktail still needed something austere and unique, with a bit of character." Now Klus makes the drink with the spicy, citrusy, rum-like spirit Batavia-Arrack, a popular ingredient among US mixologists.

1½ ounces apple brandy, preferably Laird's bonded
¾ ounce Batavia-Arrack van Oosten
¾ ounce fresh lemon juice
¾ ounce honey syrup (1 tablespoon honey mixed with ½ tablespoon warm water)
Dash of Angostura bitters
Ice
¾ ounce chilled sparkling dry white wine
Pinch of cinnamon, for garnish

In a cocktail shaker, combine the brandy, Batavia-Arrack, lemon juice, honey syrup and bitters. Fill the shaker with ice and shake well. Strain into a chilled white wine glass, top with the wine and garnish with the cinnamon.
—*Tommy Klus*

APPLE THIEF *

ALLOW 8 DAYS FOR
STEEPING

*"The Apple Thief is
perfect for times when a
Manhattan is too rich
and a martini is too dry,"
Klus says. The base spir-
its are Calvados, an aged
brandy distilled from
apple cider; and single-
malt Scotch with a rich,
buttery flavor (such as
Glenmorangie 10 year).
Any leftover Brown
Sugar–Fig Syrup would
be delicious drizzled over
ice cream.*

*For a mocktail variation,
see **P.160.***

1¼ ounces Calvados
¾ ounce Scotch, preferably single malt
½ ounce gin
½ ounce Brown Sugar–Fig Syrup (below)
Dash of Fee Brothers Old Fashion aromatic bitters
Ice
1 lemon twist, for garnish

In a mixing glass, combine the Calvados, Scotch, gin, Brown Sugar–Fig Syrup and bitters; fill with ice and stir well. Strain into a chilled coupe and garnish with the lemon twist. —*TK*

BROWN SUGAR–FIG SYRUP

In a small heatproof bowl, combine 2 ounces (¼ cup plus 2 tablespoons) dried figs with ¼ cup dark brown sugar and mix well. Cover the bowl and let stand at room temperature for 24 hours. Stir in 6 ounces hot water, cover and let steep in the refrigerator for 1 week. Strain the syrup into a jar, cover and refrigerate for up to 2 weeks. Makes about 6 ounces.

BACCHANALIAN

Chris Hannah of Arnaud's French 75 Bar in New Orleans loves serving this drink in the fall and winter—especially during Mardi Gras and the carnival season in New Orleans (January to March).

1¾ ounces VS Cognac
¾ ounce fruity red wine, such as Claret or Merlot
½ ounce fresh lemon juice
½ ounce light brown sugar syrup
    (½ tablespoon light brown sugar mixed
    with ½ tablespoon warm water)
Ice
Pinch of freshly grated nutmeg, for garnish

In a cocktail shaker, combine the Cognac, wine, lemon juice and brown sugar syrup. Fill the shaker with ice and shake well. Strain into a chilled ice-filled red wine glass and garnish with the nutmeg. —*Chris Hannah*

ELYSIAN FIELDS

Hannah adds a good dose of Peychaud's bitters here, giving the cocktail a pretty pink-red color. Peychaud's, a brand of bitters with bright anise and cherry flavors, is made from a recipe dating back to 19th-century New Orleans.

2 ounces VS Cognac
¼ ounce maraschino liqueur
¼ ounce yellow Chartreuse (spicy herbal liqueur)
¼ ounce Peychaud's bitters
½ ounce fresh orange juice
Ice
1 lemon twist, for garnish

In a cocktail shaker, combine the Cognac, maraschino liqueur, yellow Chartreuse, Peychaud's bitters and orange juice. Fill the shaker with ice and shake well. Strain into a chilled coupe and garnish with the lemon twist. —*CH*

BACCHANALIAN
"Otto" glass by Gottfried Palatin
for Theresienthal from TableArt.

LA BELLE FEMME

This absinthe-accented drink won Hannah a trip to the Cognac region of France, where he made it for the Cognac Blues Passions festival. "The festival featured Trombone Shorty and other New Orleans bands," he says. "Pretty funny how I flew all that way to hear the songs I hear every day in New Orleans."

1¾ ounces VSOP Cognac
¾ ounce Dubonnet rouge
½ ounce Aperol
¼ ounce absinthe verte
Ice
1 lemon twist, for garnish

In a mixing glass, combine the Cognac, Dubonnet, Aperol and absinthe; fill with ice and stir well. Strain into a chilled coupe and garnish with the twist. —*Chris Hannah*

CHARENTE HESSIAN

MAKES 6 TO 8
SERVINGS

This hot Cognac punch evokes the flavors of fall. It's mixed with a pumpkin butter that includes pureed pumpkin, brown sugar, amaro and baking spices. For a quick substitute, Hannah sometimes uses a jarred pumpkin butter produced by The Fresh Market (thefresh-market.com).

PUMPKIN BUTTER

10 ounces pumpkin puree
4 tablespoons light brown sugar
4 tablespoons granulated sugar
2½ ounces apple juice
1 ounce each of amaro and fresh lemon juice
½ teaspoon cinnamon
¼ teaspoon each of ground allspice and ground cloves

PUNCH

12 ounces VS Cognac
3 ounces dry orange curaçao
1½ ounces St. Elizabeth allspice dram
6 to 8 cinnamon sticks, for garnish

In a food processor, puree the pumpkin butter ingredients. Transfer to a large heatproof bowl; stir in 24 ounces hot water and the Cognac, curaçao and allspice dram. Ladle into warmed mugs; garnish with cinnamon sticks. —*CH*

BEHIND THE FAÇADE

📷 PAGE 127

Nicole Lebedevitch, bar manager at The Hawthorne in Boston, creates this highball with Armagnac, a robust brandy produced in the Armagnac region of Gascony, France. "You'd think the bold flavors of apricot liqueur, fortified wine and bitters would mask the nuances of Armagnac in this cocktail," she says, "but the Armagnac comes through."

1½ ounces Armagnac, preferably VSOP
½ ounce apricot liqueur
½ ounce Bonal Gentiane-Quina (fortified, slightly bitter aperitif wine)
½ ounce fresh lemon juice
Dash of orange bitters
Ice
2 ounces chilled ginger ale
1 spiral-cut lemon twist (page 20), for garnish

In a cocktail shaker, combine the Armagnac, apricot liqueur, Bonal, lemon juice and bitters. Fill the shaker with ice and shake well. Fine-strain (**P.21**) into a chilled ice-filled highball glass, stir in the ginger ale and garnish with the lemon twist. —*Nicole Lebedevitch*

THE REBUTTAL

Lebedevitch makes the unlikely pairing of Armagnac and fresh mint work by simply stirring mint leaves into the drink, then straining them out. Muddling the mint or even shaking the drink would release too much of the mint oils.

2 ounces Armagnac, preferably XO
½ ounce dry orange curaçao
½ ounce amaro, preferably S. Maria al Monte
2¼ teaspoons Simple Syrup (page 22)
5 mint leaves
Ice

In a mixing glass, combine the Armagnac, curaçao, amaro, Simple Syrup and mint; fill with ice and stir well. Strain the drink into a chilled double rocks glass. —*NL*

PÈLERIN

Although French in name, this cocktail was designed to highlight Germain-Robin, a brandy distilled in California using high-quality wine grapes. Maple syrup and allspice liqueur give it a pronounced autumnal flavor.

1½ ounces VSOP brandy, preferably Germain-Robin

¾ teaspoon St. Elizabeth allspice dram (rum-based allspice liqueur)

1 ounce fresh lemon juice

¾ ounce pure maple syrup

Dash of Angostura bitters

Ice

In a cocktail shaker, combine the brandy, allspice dram, lemon juice, maple syrup and bitters. Fill the shaker with ice and shake well. Fine-strain (**P.21**) into a chilled coupe. —*Nicole Lebedevitch*

CONSTANT TRAVELER

This warming cold-weather drink features Armagnac, crème de cacao and a sweet, thyme-infused Madeira syrup. It's an unconventional combination that is surprisingly delicious.

1½ ounces Armagnac, preferably VSOP

¾ ounce Madeira Syrup (below)

¼ ounce white crème de cacao

3 ounces hot brewed coffee

In a warmed mug or heatproof glass, stir the Armagnac with the Madeira Syrup and crème de cacao until combined. Top with the coffee. —*NL*

MADEIRA SYRUP

In a small saucepan, combine 6 ounces Sercial Madeira with ¼ cup honey and 1 thyme sprig. Simmer over low heat, stirring, just until the honey darkens, about 5 minutes. Remove from the heat, cover and let stand for 15 minutes. Let the syrup cool, then strain into a jar. Cover and refrigerate for up to 1 week. Makes about 4 ounces.

NIPO–PERUANA*

Los Angeles mixologist Lindsay Nader improves on the Midori Sour, which can be cloyingly sweet. To cut some of the intensity of the melon liqueur, she adds Peruvian pisco— a clear brandy distilled from grapes—along with lemon and lime juice.

For a mocktail variation, see **P.166.*

1½ ounces pisco, preferably Peruvian
½ ounce melon liqueur
½ ounce fresh lemon juice
½ ounce fresh lime juice
½ ounce orgeat (almond-flavored syrup)
Ice
3 honeydew melon balls skewered on a pick, for garnish

In a cocktail shaker, combine the pisco, melon liqueur, citrus juices and orgeat. Fill the shaker with ice and shake well. Strain into a chilled coupe and garnish with the skewered honeydew balls. —*Lindsay Nader*

NORWEGIAN EMBASSY

This potent drink combines pisco with Norwegian aged aquavit, honey and a good amount of orange flower water. The result is an aromatic cocktail that is silky, spicy and floral.

2½ ounces pisco, preferably Peruvian
¼ ounce aged aquavit, preferably Linie
¾ teaspoon honey
5 dashes of orange flower water
Dash of Angostura bitters
Ice
1 organic orchid, nasturtium or other edible flower, for garnish (optional)

In a mixing glass, combine the pisco, aquavit, honey, orange flower water and bitters; fill with ice and stir well. Strain into a chilled coupe and garnish with the flower. —*LN*

NIPO-PERUANA

"Savoy" Champagne saucers from LSA International.

CAPTAIN COCKTAIL 🍸

El Capitán, or The Captain, is one of the most popular pisco drinks in Peru. According to Peruvian legend, military captains would ride on horseback through the Altiplano in the 1800s and drink pisco mixed with vermouth to quench their thirst. Nader's variation includes sliced red onion for complexity.

2 thin red onion slivers, plus 1 thin red onion
   wedge for garnish
1½ ounces pisco, preferably Peruvian
1½ ounces sweet vermouth,
   preferably Cocchi Vermouth di Torino
2 dashes of Angostura bitters
Ice

In a mixing glass, gently muddle the onion slivers with the pisco, vermouth and bitters; fill the glass with ice and stir well. Strain into a chilled coupe and garnish with the red onion wedge. —*Lindsay Nader*

I KNOW WHAT YOU DID LAST SUMMER

Although Peru claims to have invented pisco, here Nader prefers to use the Chilean pisco Kappa, with its citrus and honeysuckle aromas. She dry-shakes the ingredients (without ice) to incorporate the sweetened condensed milk, then serves the drink over ice.

2 ounces pisco, preferably Chilean
½ ounce sweetened condensed milk
½ ounce mango puree (store-bought or made from
   frozen mango cubes pureed in a food processor)
¼ ounce fresh lime juice
3 dashes of Angostura bitters
Ice
1 fresh mango fan or slice, for garnish

In a cocktail shaker, combine all of the ingredients except ice and the garnish; shake vigorously. Strain into a chilled ice-filled rocks glass and garnish with the mango. —*LN*

CAPTAIN COCKTAIL

"Vita" tall coupe from William Yeoward.

SPREZZATURA ROYALE **P.148**

"Facet" glasses by Lalique; "Montgomery"
cocktail shaker by Ralph Lauren; "Fuoco"
wallpaper by Trove.

LIQUEURS
& FORTIFIED WINES

DRINKS BY:

JOAQUÍN SIMÓ & TROY SIDLE • POURING RIBBONS • NEW YORK CITY

MELISSA HAYES • HOLEMAN & FINCH • ATLANTA

KIRK ESTOPINAL • CURE AND BELLOCQ • NEW ORLEANS

PO PO PUNCH

MAKES 6 SERVINGS

ALLOW FOR OVERNIGHT
MACERATING AND
2 HOURS OF CHILLING

This citrusy, tiki-style punch is from Joaquín Simó of Manhattan's Pouring Ribbons. It features orange-spiced Ramazzotti amaro (a bittersweet herbal Italian digestif) and homemade orange cordial. "Orange juice is usually the weak link in the citrus family," Simó says. *"It's kind of watery and bland, so we came up with this brighter cordial that can also be mixed into mimosas or sparkling water."*

ORANGE CORDIAL

1 large orange

¾ cup sugar

PUNCH

9 ounces Ramazzotti amaro

3 ounces bonded bourbon

3 ounces Simple Syrup (page 22)

3 ounces fresh lemon juice

6 dashes of Angostura bitters

1 big block of ice (page 20), plus crushed ice for serving

6 orange wheels and cinnamon, for garnish

1. MAKE THE CORDIAL With a vegetable peeler, peel the orange. Reserve the orange and add the peels to a small bowl along with ½ cup of the sugar. Cover and let macerate overnight, stirring occasionally.

2. The next day, stir the juice from the reserved orange into the bowl, discard the peels and whisk to dissolve the sugar. Whisk in the remaining ¼ cup of sugar until dissolved. Strain the orange cordial into a punch bowl.

3. MAKE THE PUNCH Stir in all of the remaining ingredients except the ice and garnishes. Refrigerate until chilled, about 2 hours. Stir the punch, add the big block of ice and ladle the punch into chilled crushed-ice-filled pilsner glasses; top with more crushed ice. Garnish each drink with an orange wheel and a pinch of cinnamon.

—*Joaquín Simó*

PO PO PUNCH

*"Wiener Stutzen" optic beer glass
by Lobmeyr from TableArt.*

SPREZZATURA ROYALE

📷 PAGE 145

"Sprezzatura refers to the stylishly disheveled look perfected by Italian men," says Simó. *"An artfully misknotted tie, an elegantly askew collar, mismatched socks—all done with a devil-may-care attitude."* This amaro-based sour topped with sparkling rosé embodies casual elegance.

1 ounce Amaro Nonino
½ ounce Cognac, preferably Pierre Ferrand 1840
½ ounce honey syrup (2 teaspoons honey mixed with 1 teaspoon warm water)
½ ounce fresh lemon juice
Ice
1½ ounces chilled sparkling rosé wine

In a cocktail shaker, combine the amaro, Cognac, honey syrup and lemon juice. Fill the shaker with ice and shake well. Strain into a chilled flute and top with the sparkling wine. —*Joaquín Simó*

TEDDY BEAR

Troy Sidle, Simó's partner at Pouring Ribbons, makes this drink with intensely smoky Bowmore Legend Scotch. "Troy takes an aggressively peaty Scotch and transforms it with berries and CioCiaro, a bitter orange–laced amaro," Simo says. *"The result is a bracing, approachable highball with universal appeal."* To temper the smokiness, you can substitute a less peaty Scotch like Glenlivet.

3 blackberries, plus 3 blackberries skewered on a pick for garnish
½ ounce Rich Simple Syrup (page 22)
2 ounces Amaro CioCiaro
¾ ounce single-malt Scotch
¼ ounce cream sherry
2 dashes of Angostura bitters
Ice
¾ ounce chilled club soda

In a cocktail shaker, muddle the 3 blackberries with the Rich Simple Syrup. Add the amaro, Scotch, sherry and bitters, fill the shaker with ice and shake well. Fine-strain (**P.21**) into a chilled ice-filled highball glass, stir in the club soda and garnish with the skewered blackberries. —*Troy Sidle*

MUTINY SUPPRESSOR

The base for the Mutiny Suppressor is the wonderfully complex Nardini amaro, which is infused with bitter oranges and peppermint and tastes of licorice. Simó adds a bit of Navy-strength gin, a potent style of the spirit amped up to 57 percent alcohol. "A little can go a long way," Simó says.

1 ounce Amaro Nardini
½ ounce Punt e Mes (spicy, orange-accented sweet vermouth from Italy)
½ ounce Navy-strength gin, preferably Perry's Tot
¼ ounce Galliano (Italian herbal liqueur)
Ice, plus 1 large ice cube (page 20) for serving
1 grapefruit twist, for garnish

In a mixing glass, combine the amaro, Punt e Mes, gin and Galliano; fill with ice and stir well. Strain into a chilled rocks glass over the large ice cube and garnish with the grapefruit twist. —JS

FRIAR FLIP

In cocktail terminology, a flip is a sweetened drink made with a spirit, whole egg and spice (typically nutmeg). The Friar Flip from Melissa Hayes of Holeman & Finch in Atlanta gets its spice from chocolaty mole bitters and yellow Chartreuse, a honeyed herbal liqueur made by Carthusian monks since the 1700s.

1 ounce yellow Chartreuse
½ ounce Bonal Gentiane-Quina (fortified, slightly bitter aperitif wine)
½ ounce Simple Syrup (page 22)
½ ounce fresh lemon juice
4 dashes of Bittermens Xocolatl Mole bitters
Pinch of salt
1 large egg
Ice
Pinch of freshly grated nutmeg, for garnish

In a cocktail shaker, combine all of the ingredients except ice and the garnish and shake vigorously. Fill the shaker with ice and shake again. Strain into a chilled coupe and garnish with the nutmeg. —Melissa Hayes

SO SAY KAISER

Hayes combines two ingredients that aren't often mixed together: the spicy, fruity, gin-based aperitif Pimm's and the honeyed, Scotch-based liqueur Drambuie. They create an elegant, pleasantly bittersweet cocktail.

1 ounce Pimm's No. 1
½ ounce Drambuie
½ ounce Cocchi Americano
   (fortified, slightly bitter aperitif wine)
¼ ounce Averna amaro (bittersweet herbal digestif)
¾ ounce fresh lemon juice
Dash of celery bitters
Ice
1 lemon twist, flamed (page 20), for garnish

In a cocktail shaker, combine all of the ingredients except ice and the garnish. Fill the shaker with ice and shake well. Strain into a chilled coupe and garnish with the flamed lemon twist. —*Melissa Hayes*

SO SAY KAISER

"Dagny" Champagne glass by Ralph Lauren.

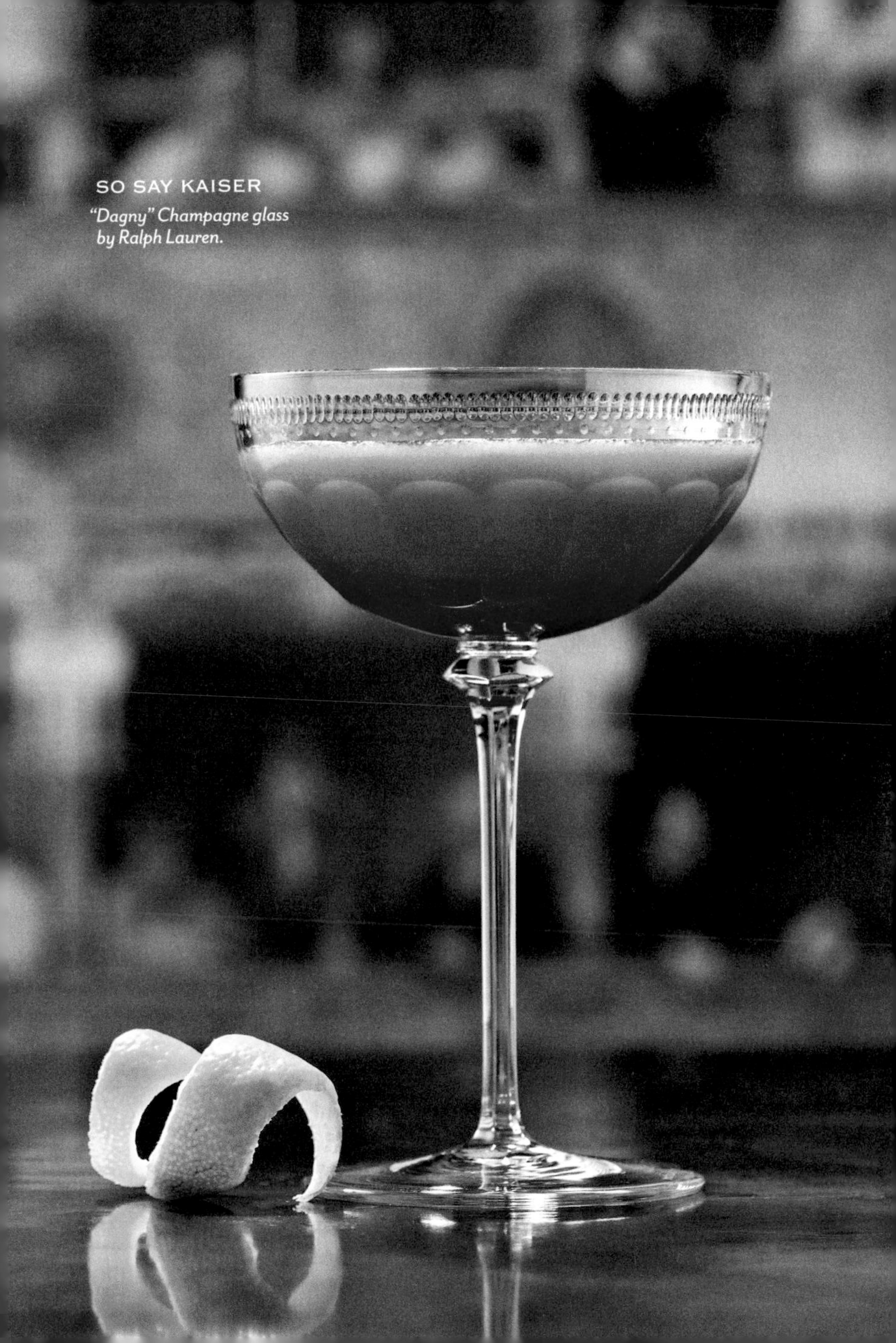

CHEER CAMP

The cherry liqueur–based Cheer Camp reminds Hayes of one of her favorite sodas, Cheerwine, a cherry-flavored soft drink popular in the South. "The cocktail's cherries, cocoa and egg white meringue also remind me of milk shakes and cotton candy," she says.

1½ ounces Heering cherry liqueur
½ ounce Suze (French gentian aperitif)
¾ ounce fresh lime juice
1 large egg white
Ice
1½ ounces chilled dry sparkling wine, such as cava
Pinch of unsweetened dark cocoa powder, for garnish

In a cocktail shaker, combine the Heering, Suze, lime juice and egg white and shake vigorously; fill with ice and shake again. Strain into a chilled ice-filled rocks glass, top with the sparkling wine and garnish. —*Melissa Hayes*

THE VEILED INSULT

Hayes came up with this drink when two of her bartender friends asked for a "dealer's choice" drink at a bar and felt slighted by getting the commonplace Blood and Sand (Scotch, vermouth, cherry liqueur and orange juice). She created this variation in their honor, replacing the Scotch with the herbal liqueur Bénédictine.

1½ ounces Bénédictine
½ ounce sour cherry liqueur, preferably Leopold Bros. Michigan Tart Cherry liqueur
¼ ounce Fernet-Branca (bitter Italian digestif)
¾ ounce fresh lemon juice
½ ounce fresh orange juice
4 dashes of Angostura bitters
Ice, plus 1 large ice cube (page 20) for serving
1 orange twist
1 mint sprig, for garnish

In a cocktail shaker, combine the Bénédictine, sour cherry liqueur, Fernet-Branca, citrus juices and bitters. Fill the shaker with ice and shake well. Strain into a chilled rocks glass over the large ice cube. Pinch the twist over the drink and discard, then garnish with the mint sprig. —*MH*

CHEER CAMP

*"Ginette" tumbler by Sugahara
from Dandelion.*

CHERI CHERI

The funky flavors in this cocktail by Kirk Estopinal of Cure and Bellocq in New Orleans come from manzanilla sherry en rama. Sherries are usually completely filtered before bottling, but en rama sherries are only lightly filtered.

1½ ounces manzanilla sherry, preferably *en rama*
¾ ounce Batavia-Arrack van Oosten (spicy, citrusy, rum-like spirit from Java)
¼ ounce orgeat (almond-flavored syrup)
3 drops of Fee Brothers Old Fashion aromatic bitters
Ice
Small pinch of freshly grated nutmeg, for garnish

In a mixing glass, combine the sherry, Batavia-Arrack, orgeat and bitters; fill with ice and stir well. Strain into a chilled coupe and garnish with the nutmeg.
—*Kirk Estopinal*

THE SEA DOG

People often associate the fortified wine Madeira with syrupy-sweet flavors, but good-quality Madeira is complex and delicious, with a wonderful acidity. The Sercial Madeira that Estopinal uses here is the driest style.

2 ounces Sercial Madeira
½ ounce Simple Syrup (page 22)
Dash of Bittermens Xocolatl Mole bitters
2 orange twists
Ice cubes, plus cracked ice for serving
1 lemon twist, for garnish

In a cocktail shaker, combine the Madeira, Simple Syrup, bitters and orange twists. Fill the shaker with ice cubes and shake well. Strain into a chilled cracked-ice-filled double rocks glass and garnish with the lemon twist. —*KE*

CHERI CHERI
"3/62" Champagne bowl by Nason Moretti from TableArt.

MAURY'S COBBLER

*Estopinal uses a forti-
fied French dessert wine
like Maury or Banyuls
(made from red Grenache
grapes and named for
their regions of produc-
tion) as the base for this
sweet, punch-like cock-
tail. "Maury and Banyuls
remind me of being out-
side," he says. "This drink
makes them refreshing
enough for New Orleans
summers."*

2 ounces fortified French red dessert wine,
   preferably Maury or Banyuls
½ ounce Simple Syrup (page 22)
3 orange wedges
Ice cubes, plus crushed ice for serving
1 orange wheel, halved, and ¼ ounce high-proof
   Jamaican rum, for garnish

In a cocktail shaker, combine the wine, Simple Syrup and
orange wedges. Fill the shaker with ice cubes and shake
well. Strain into a chilled crushed-ice-filled julep cup.
Garnish with the orange wheel halves, then pour the rum
over them. —*Kirk Estopinal*

TAWNY LITTLE BLOOD

*Estopinal riffs on the
spicy, citrusy Mexican
drink called sangrita
using rich, nutty tawny
port and mezcal. "The
smoke and brine in mez-
cal love port," he says.*

2 ounces tawny port
¾ ounce mezcal
1 ounce fresh orange juice
¾ ounce fresh grapefruit juice
½ ounce cold water
20 drops of Bittermens
    Hellfire Habanero Shrub bitters
1 jalapeño slice
Pinch of flaky sea salt
1 ice cube, for serving
1 lime wheel and ½ orange wheel, for garnish

In a mixing glass, combine all of the ingredients except
the ice cube and garnishes. Stir until the salt dissolves.
Strain into a chilled rocks glass, add the ice cube and
garnish with the lime and orange wheels. —*KE*

TAWNY LITTLE BLOOD
"Herringbone" glass by Artël (in background).

MOCKTAILS

MIXOLOGIST JOHN DEBARY OF NYC'S PDT AND MOMOFUKU, AND **F&W COCKTAILS** ASSISTANT EDITOR, TESTED ALL OF THE DRINK RECIPES IN THIS BOOK. THE MOCKTAILS THAT HE CREATED HERE ARE VARIATIONS ON COCKTAILS THROUGHOUT THE BOOK.

LUCHADOR'S
DAUGHTER P.163

*"Margherita" glasses by Missoni
from Replacements.*

APPLE GIVER

"Mocktails are a fun challenge. The goal is to re-create the thrill and complexity of a cocktail," says deBary. His revamp of the Apple Thief (**P.133**) replaces Calvados with apple cider.

(Note: The bitters here are alcohol-based. For a completely nonalcoholic cocktail, leave them out.)

2 ounces chilled unsweetened apple cider
1 ounce Brown Sugar–Fig Syrup (page 133)
2 dashes of Fee Brothers
  Old Fashion aromatic bitters (optional)
Ice
1 lemon twist, for garnish

In a cocktail shaker, combine the cider, fig syrup and bitters. Fill the shaker with ice and shake well. Strain into a chilled coupe and garnish with the lemon twist.

BLACK & COPPER

Based on the Black & Gold vodka-strawberry cocktail (**P.46**), the Black & Copper balances the sweet-tart flavors of aged balsamic and strawberries with spicy black pepper.

4 strawberries, quartered,
  plus 1 halved strawberry for garnish
¾ ounce Black Pepper Syrup (page 46)
¾ ounce fresh lemon juice
¼ ounce aged balsamic vinegar
Ice
1 ounce chilled club soda

In a cocktail shaker, muddle the 4 quartered strawberries with the Black Pepper Syrup. Add the lemon juice and vinegar, then fill the shaker with ice and shake well. Fine-strain (**P.21**) the drink into a chilled coupe, stir in the club soda and garnish with the halved strawberry.

BLACK & COPPER

*"Davina" Champagne saucer
by William Yeoward; "Primate
in Pomp" tray (in background)
from Michele Varian.*

GRAPES OF REDEMPTION

*This nonalcoholic version of the mezcal-based Grapes of Wrath (**P.84**) tastes like grape soda for grown-ups.*

30 Concord grapes
1 ounce Vanilla Simple Syrup (page 22)
¼ ounce fresh lime juice
Crushed ice
4 ounces chilled club soda

In a mixing glass, muddle the Concord grapes with the Vanilla Simple Syrup and lime juice. Fill a chilled rocks glass with crushed ice, add the club soda, then top with more crushed ice. Pour the grape mixture on top.

LOWLAND TODDY

*DeBary uses ginger syrup and licorice tea to create this mocktail rendition of his Scotch whisky–based Highland Toddy (**P.125**).*

½ ounce Ginger Syrup (page 130)
1 licorice tea bag
4 dried chamomile flowers or 1 chamomile tea bag
1 rosemary sprig
8 ounces boiling water
1 lemon wedge

In a warmed mug or heatproof glass, combine the Ginger Syrup, licorice tea bag, chamomile flowers and rosemary sprig. Pour the boiling water on top and let steep for 5 minutes. Press the liquid from the tea bag and remove the bag, the chamomile flowers and the rosemary sprig. Squeeze the lemon wedge over the drink and drop it in.

LUCHADOR'S DAUGHTER

📷 PAGE 159

*The hibiscus tea in this colorful, virgin take on the tequila cocktail Luchador's Lady (**P.78**) provides a tannic edge that is reminiscent of red wine. The mocktail is sweetened with a caramelized sugar-and-**pineapple** syrup spiced with cinnamon and vanilla.*

1½ ounces chilled brewed hibiscus tea
1 ounce fresh lime juice
1 ounce Caramelized-Pineapple Syrup (page 78)
1 large egg white
Ice
2 ounces chilled club soda
Pinch of cinnamon, for garnish

In a cocktail shaker, combine the hibiscus tea, lime juice, Caramelized-Pineapple Syrup and egg white and shake vigorously. Fill the shaker with ice and shake again. Strain into a chilled highball glass, top with the club soda and garnish with the cinnamon.

THIRD LEFT

*This remake of the vodka cocktail Second Left (**P.50**) includes blood orange marmalade, Italian orange soda and sherry vinegar, which gives the drink a wonderful tanginess.*

1½   tablespoons blood orange marmalade
¾   ounce fresh lemon juice
½   ounce Simple Syrup (page 22)
½   ounce sherry vinegar
Ice
4   ounces chilled Italian orange soda, such as San Pellegrino Aranciata

In a cocktail shaker, combine the marmalade, lemon juice, Simple Syrup and vinegar. Fill the shaker with ice and shake well. Strain into a chilled ice-filled collins glass and stir in the orange soda.

SAILING OFF

*Heat seekers will love this spicy ginger beer drink, which gets an extra kick from habanero-infused honey. The honey-habanero syrup recipe is from Sean Kenyon of Williams & Graham in Denver, whose spiced-rum Sailing On (**P.98**) inspired this mocktail.*

1½   ounces fresh lemon juice
½   ounce Honey-Habanero Syrup (below)
1   tablespoon apricot preserves
Ice
1   ounce chilled ginger beer

In a cocktail shaker, combine the lemon juice, Honey-Habanero Syrup and preserves. Fill the shaker with ice and shake well. Strain into a chilled coupe and top with the ginger beer.

HONEY-HABANERO SYRUP

In a small saucepan, combine 1 cup each of honey and water and ½ teaspoon dried habanero (available at Latin markets); bring to a boil. Simmer over low heat for about 10 minutes, then let cool. Strain the syrup into a jar and refrigerate for up to 1 month. Makes about 11 ounces.

THIRD LEFT
"Corinne" glass by William Yeoward.

ROYAL MONDAY MORNING

*Adapted from the vermouth-based Royal Sunday Morning (**P.29**), this pretty pink drink is best made with a not-too-sweet grapefruit soda like GuS or the nicely bitter San Pellegrino Pompelmo.*

1 ounce fresh grapefruit juice
1 tablespoon raspberry preserves
Ice
3 ounces chilled club soda
2 ounces chilled Italian grapefruit soda, such as San Pellegrino Pompelmo

In a cocktail shaker, combine the grapefruit juice and preserves. Fill the shaker with ice and shake well. Strain into a chilled flute or coupe and top with both sodas.

NIPO-PERUANA (PG 13)

*In this mocktail version of the pisco-based Nipo-Peruana (**P.140**), fresh honeydew juice stands in for melon liqueur.*

One 3½-pound honeydew melon, halved and seeded (for 2 ounces fresh honeydew juice)
¾ ounce fresh lemon juice
¾ ounce fresh lime juice
½ ounce orgeat (almond-flavored syrup)
Ice
3 honeydew melon balls skewered on a pick, for garnish

Chop the melon flesh and transfer to a blender. Puree until smooth. Strain the puree, without pressing on the solids, to extract clear green juice. Reserve 2 ounces of the juice and refrigerate the rest for another use. In a cocktail shaker, combine the 2 ounces melon juice with the citrus juices and orgeat. Fill the shaker with ice and shake well. Strain into a chilled coupe and garnish with the skewered melon balls.

ROYAL MONDAY MORNING
"Night Sky" toasting glasses from BHLDN.

SWEET BABY SWIZZLE

This tropical drink is a variation on the rhum agricole cocktail Sweet Mary Swizzle (P.101). The soursop juice has a creamy flavor that's reminiscent of bananas or coconut, with a bit of citrusy tartness.

2 ounces chilled soursop juice (see Note)
1 ounce chilled unsweetened pineapple juice
½ ounce fresh lemon juice
Pinch of ground cloves
Crushed ice
1 mint sprig, for garnish

In a chilled collins glass, combine the 3 juices and the cloves. Fill the glass with crushed ice and mix by spinning a swizzle stick or bar spoon between your hands. Top with more crushed ice and garnish with the mint sprig.

NOTE Soursop juice, which is made from a tropical fruit of the same name, is available at Latin and specialty food markets and *amazon.com.*

N⊚ZILLA

The spiced pineapple syrup here is from San Francisco mixologist Mathias Simonis, whose @N8Zilla rum drink (P.90) inspired this mocktail. Steeped with cloves, allspice, peppercorns and vanilla, the syrup replaces the flavors lost by omitting the rum.

(Note: The bitters here are alcohol-based. For a completely nonalcoholic cocktail, leave them out.)

2 ounces fresh orange juice
1¾ ounces Spiced Pineapple Syrup (page 90)
1 ounce fresh lemon juice
½ ounce fresh lime juice
3 dashes of chocolate bitters (optional)
Crushed ice
1 pineapple wedge and 1 maraschino cherry, for garnish

In a cocktail shaker, combine the orange juice, Spiced Pineapple Syrup, lemon and lime juices and bitters. Fill the shaker with crushed ice and shake well. Pour (don't strain) into a chilled tiki mug and garnish the drink with the pineapple wedge and cherry.

SWEET BABY SWIZZLE
"Drift Ice" glass by Moser.

PARTY FOOD

KANSAI KICK **P.122**

SHRIMP GYOZA **P.186**

Platter by Heath Ceramics.

TOTAL: 30 MIN PLUS COOLING • MAKES 20 CUPS

ENDLESS CARAMEL CORN

Salty, sweet and amazingly crisp, this caramel-coated popcorn gets a hit of spice from the adobo sauce in canned chipotles.

3 tablespoons vegetable oil, plus more for greasing
½ cup popping corn
1½ teaspoons baking soda
1 teaspoon adobo sauce (from a can of chipotle chiles in adobo)
3 cups sugar
3 tablespoons unsalted butter
1 tablespoon kosher salt

1. Lightly coat a large bowl and 2 large rimmed baking sheets with oil. In a large saucepan, combine the 3 tablespoons of oil and the popping corn. Cover and cook over moderate heat until the corn starts to pop. Shake the pan and cook until the corn stops popping, about 5 minutes. Transfer the popcorn to the prepared bowl.

2. In a small bowl, whisk the baking soda with the adobo sauce. In a large saucepan, combine the sugar with the butter, salt and ½ cup of water and bring to a boil, stirring until the sugar dissolves. Boil over moderate heat without stirring until a golden caramel forms, about 13 minutes. Remove from the heat and stir in the adobo mixture; the syrup will foam. Immediately drizzle the hot caramel over the popcorn and, using 2 greased spoons, toss to coat. Spread the caramel corn on the prepared baking sheets in an even layer and let cool completely before serving. —*Stephen Jones*

MAKE AHEAD The caramel corn can be stored in an airtight container for up to 5 days.

**BLUE HOUND
KITCHEN & COCKTAILS**
2 E. Jefferson St.
Phoenix • 602-258-0231
bluehoundkitchen.com

ENDLESS
CARAMEL CORN

CASTING ASPERSIONS
P.112

ACTIVE: 10 MIN; TOTAL: 50 MIN • MAKES 4 CUPS

CREOLE BEER NUTS

These not-too-sweet pecans are coated with a potent mix of garlic powder, cayenne and dried herbs. Beaten egg white creates a terrific crust on the nuts as they bake.

1 **large egg white**

2 **tablespoons sugar**

4 **cups pecan halves (14 ounces)**

1 **tablespoon kosher salt**

2 **teaspoons cayenne pepper**

2 **teaspoons sweet paprika**

2 **teaspoons Creole seasoning (see Note)**

1. Preheat the oven to 300° and line a rimmed baking sheet with parchment paper. In a large bowl, beat the egg white with an electric mixer until foamy. Add 1 tablespoon of the sugar and beat at high speed until firm peaks form, about 1 minute. Add the pecans and toss to coat. Spread the pecans on the prepared baking sheet and bake for 10 minutes, until the nuts are just slightly dry.

2. Meanwhile, in another large bowl, whisk the salt with the cayenne, paprika, Creole seasoning and the remaining 1 tablespoon of sugar. Add the pecans and toss well. Return the pecans to the baking sheet and bake for about 30 minutes longer, stirring every 10 minutes, until golden and dry. Let cool completely before serving.
—*Juan Carlos Gonzalez*

NOTE Creole seasoning is a blend of spices popular in Louisiana cooking that often includes paprika, garlic powder, onion powder, cayenne pepper and dried herbs like oregano and thyme. It is available at most grocery stores and online at *amazon.com.*

MAKE AHEAD The Creole Beer Nuts can be stored in an airtight container for up to 1 week.

SOBOU

310 Chartres St.
New Orleans
504-552-4095
sobounola.com

TOTAL: 15 MIN • MAKES 4 TO 6 SERVINGS

GUACAMOLE WITH PICKLED JALAPEÑOS

Chef Alex Stupak makes extraordinary guacamoles for his two New York City restaurants, Empellón Taqueria and Empellón Cocina. Here, he cleverly mixes in pickled jalapeños, which add both heat and tang to the mashed avocados.

2 Hass avocados, halved and pitted
¼ cup chopped cilantro
3 tablespoons minced white onion
2 pickled jalapeños, stemmed and finely chopped
1 tablespoon fresh lime juice
Sea salt
Tortilla chips, for serving

Scoop the avocados into a medium bowl and coarsely mash with a fork. Fold in the cilantro, onion, jalapeños and lime juice and season with salt. Serve with tortilla chips.
—*Alex Stupak*

EMPELLÓN TAQUERIA
230 W. Fourth St.
New York City
212-367-0999
empellon.com

TOTAL: 30 MIN • MAKES 4 TO 6 SERVINGS

BACON-WRAPPED CHERRY PEPPERS

These genius hors d'oeuvres from Bluestem chef Colby Garrelts require just three ingredients. They can be prepped ahead of time, so they're great to serve at parties.

6   jarred hot cherry peppers—halved through the stem, seeded, drained and patted dry
⅓   cup cream cheese, softened
12   thin bacon slices (6 ounces)

1. Preheat the oven to 350°. Stuff each cherry pepper half with a heaping teaspoon of cream cheese and wrap with a slice of bacon; secure with a toothpick.

2. Arrange the stuffed peppers in a large ovenproof skillet and cook over moderate heat, turning, until the bacon is browned, 12 to 15 minutes. Transfer the skillet to the oven and bake for about 5 minutes, until the bacon is crisp and the cream cheese is hot. Serve warm. —*Colby Garrelts*

BLUESTEM
900 Westport Rd.
Kansas City, MO
816-561-1101
bluestemkc.com

BACON-WRAPPED
CHERRY PEPPERS

ACTIVE: 30 MIN; TOTAL: 1 HR • MAKES 8 SERVINGS

CREAMY, CHEESY ARTICHOKE DIP

Chef Michael White's version of the classic cheesy, warm dip makes great use of frozen artichokes: They're simmered with garlic and wine; mixed with cream cheese, Gruyère and Tabasco; and baked with a panko bread crumb topping. For extra crunch, White likes to sprinkle fried shallots on top.

2 tablespoons extra-virgin olive oil
1 large shallot, minced
2 garlic cloves, minced
One 9-ounce package frozen artichoke
    hearts, thawed and drained
¼ cup dry white wine
8 ounces cream cheese, softened
1 cup shredded Gruyère cheese (3 ounces)
2 tablespoons finely chopped parsley
1½ tablespoons fresh lemon juice
1 teaspoon Tabasco
½ cup plus 2 tablespoons freshly grated
    Parmigiano-Reggiano cheese
Kosher salt and freshly ground pepper
¼ cup panko (Japanese bread crumbs)
Toast points and assorted crudités, such as red bell
    pepper strips and fennel wedges, for serving

1. Preheat the oven to 400°. In a skillet, heat the oil. Add the shallot and garlic and cook over moderate heat, stirring, until softened, about 3 minutes. Add the artichoke hearts and cook, stirring, until heated through, about 5 minutes. Add the wine and simmer until most of the liquid has evaporated, about 3 minutes; let cool.

2. In a bowl, combine the cream cheese, Gruyère, parsley, lemon juice, Tabasco and ½ cup of the Parmigiano. Fold in the artichoke mixture and season with salt and pepper. Scrape into a shallow 3-cup baking dish and sprinkle the panko and remaining Parmigiano on top. Bake for about 20 minutes, until heated through and lightly golden on top. Serve with toast points and crudités. —*Michael White*

THE BUTTERFLY*

225 West Broadway
New York City
thebutterflynyc.com
* To open spring 2013

ACTIVE: 30 MIN; TOTAL: 1 HR • MAKES 4 TO 6 SERVINGS

MANCHEGO FRITTERS

These croquettes from chef Carmen González were inspired by almojábanas, Puerto Rican fritters made with rice flour and mild white cheese. "My Auntie Nega made the best almojábanas I ever tasted," González says. "As kids we would fight over them." Like her aunt's, González's fritters are crisp on the outside, melty on the inside.

1 cup all-purpose flour

1 teaspoon baking powder

2 large eggs, lightly beaten

½ cup whole milk

2 tablespoons unsalted butter

1 teaspoon kosher salt, plus more for sprinkling

4 ounces Manchego cheese, shredded

Canola oil, for frying

Hot sauce, for serving

1. In a medium bowl, whisk the flour with the baking powder and eggs. In a medium saucepan, bring the milk to a simmer with the butter and the 1 teaspoon of salt. Remove from the heat and gradually stir the warm milk into the flour mixture until smooth.

2. Wipe out the saucepan. Scrape the batter into the pan and cook over moderately low heat, stirring constantly, until the batter starts to pull away from the side of the pan, about 10 minutes. Remove from the heat and stir in the shredded cheese; let cool.

3. Line a baking sheet with wax paper. Scoop level tablespoons of the batter onto the baking sheet and roll them into balls. Refrigerate until firm, about 15 minutes.

4. In a saucepan, heat 2 inches of oil to 350°. Working in batches, fry the cheese balls until crisp and golden, about 4 minutes. Drain the fritters on paper towels and sprinkle with salt. Serve warm, with hot sauce. *—Carmen González*

**CARMEN AT
THE DANFORTH**
163 Danforth St.
Portland, ME
207-879-8755
danforthmaine.com

TOTAL: 45 MIN • MAKES 4 TO 6 SERVINGS

FRIED OKRA WITH JALAPEÑO JELLY

Southern cooks like Punch Bowl Social's Sergio Romero, who is from Mississippi, love serving fried dishes with sweet-spicy pepper jelly. Be sure to use fine cornmeal and tender young okra for the recipe here.

2 cups buttermilk

3 garlic cloves, smashed

½ teaspoon Tabasco

Kosher salt

1 cup all-purpose flour

1 cup fine stone-ground cornmeal

½ teaspoon cayenne pepper

½ teaspoon freshly ground black pepper

1 pound okra, stemmed (see Note)

Canola oil, for frying

Jalapeño pepper jelly, for serving

1. In a medium saucepan, combine the buttermilk, garlic, Tabasco and 1 tablespoon of salt and bring to a simmer. Remove from the heat and let steep for 10 minutes. Using a slotted spoon, remove the garlic and discard. Let the buttermilk cool completely.

2. Set a rack over a baking sheet. In a large bowl, whisk the flour with the cornmeal, cayenne, black pepper and 1½ teaspoons of salt. Dip the okra in the buttermilk, letting the excess drip back into the pan, then dredge in the cornmeal mixture. Transfer the coated okra to the rack.

3. In a large saucepan, heat 1½ inches of canola oil to 350°. Working in batches, fry the okra until golden, about 4 minutes. Using the slotted spoon, transfer the okra to paper towels to drain; sprinkle with salt. Serve the fried okra right away, with jalapeño pepper jelly.

—Sergio Romero

NOTE Cut off the stems just at the base, leaving the pods intact, to avoid producing okra's characteristic slime.

PUNCH BOWL SOCIAL

65 Broadway • Denver

303-765-2695

punchbowlsocial.com

ACTIVE: 25 MIN; TOTAL: 1 HR 15 MIN • MAKES 6 SERVINGS

NEW SHRIMP COCKTAIL

This reimagined shrimp cocktail from chef Stefan Jarausch features a vibrant horseradish cocktail sauce that includes big chunks of chopped shrimp. He reserves a few jumbo shrimp for dipping into the sauce.

1 lemon, cut into 8 wedges, plus more for garnish
1 bay leaf
1 teaspoon black peppercorns
½ teaspoon Old Bay Seasoning
Salt and freshly ground pepper
18 jumbo shrimp, shelled and deveined
1 cup ketchup
¼ cup peeled, seeded and minced cucumber
1 tablespoon minced red onion
1 tablespoon finely grated peeled fresh horseradish (or jarred horseradish), plus more for garnish
1 tablespoon fresh lemon juice
1 teaspoon finely grated lemon zest
1 serrano chile, seeded and minced
1 teaspoon Worcestershire sauce
¼ teaspoon Tabasco

1. In a large saucepan, combine 1 gallon of water with the 8 lemon wedges, the bay leaf, peppercorns, Old Bay and 1 teaspoon of salt and bring to a boil. Add the shrimp and return to a boil. Remove from the heat, cover and let the shrimp poach until just opaque throughout, about 5 minutes. Drain and rinse the shrimp with cold water, then refrigerate until chilled, 30 minutes.

2. In a medium bowl, mix all of the remaining ingredients and season with salt and pepper. Cut 12 of the shrimp into 1-inch pieces and fold them in. To serve, spoon the chopped-shrimp salad into 6 glasses or bowls and top with the remaining whole shrimp. Garnish with freshly grated horseradish and lemon wedges. —*Stefan Jarausch*

OAK LONG BAR + KITCHEN
138 St. James Ave.
Boston • 617-585-7222
oaklongbarkitchen.com

TOTAL: 45 MIN PLUS 2 HR MARINATING • MAKES 4 SERVINGS

PERUVIAN ANTICUCHOS WITH RED SALSA

Anticuchos *(grilled skewers of marinated meat) are a street-food staple in Peru. The recipe here combines cubes of hanger steak with a salsa that gets its kick from Peruvian* ají limo *chile paste.*

⅓ cup *ají panca* paste (see Note)
⅓ cup grapeseed oil
6 garlic cloves, minced
¼ cup red wine vinegar
2 teaspoons salt
2 teaspoons finely chopped oregano
1 teaspoon ground cumin
¾ teaspoon freshly ground black pepper
1 pound hanger steak, cut into 1-inch cubes
Red Salsa (below), for serving

1. In a mini food processor, combine all of the ingredients except the steak and salsa and pulse to a coarse puree. Transfer the marinade to a bowl, add the steak cubes and toss to coat. Refrigerate for 2 hours.

2. Light a grill or preheat a cast-iron griddle. Remove the steak from the marinade and thread the cubes onto small skewers, leaving a bit of space between the cubes. Grill over moderately high heat, brushing once with any remaining marinade and turning occasionally, for about 8 minutes for medium meat. Serve with the salsa. —*Erik Ramirez*

RED SALSA

In a mini food processor, pulse 1 tablespoon *ají limo* paste (see Note) with 1 chopped roasted red bell pepper until nearly smooth. Transfer to a bowl and fold in 3 minced scallions, ¼ cup chopped cilantro, 1 minced garlic clove, 2 tablespoons minced red onion, 1 tablespoon each of red wine vinegar and fresh lime juice and ¼ cup grapeseed oil. Season with salt. Makes about 1 cup.

NOTE *Ají panca* and *ají limo* chile pastes are available at specialty food shops and *spanishtable.com.*

RAYMI

43 W. 24th St.
New York City
212-929-1200
richardsandoval.com/ raymi

PERUVIAN ANTICUCHOS
WITH RED SALSA

"Candy Stripe" glass by LBK Studio.

TOTAL: 50 MIN • MAKES 12 PIECES

PANKO-COATED EGGS WITH ASIAN MUSTARD

In this updated, vegetarian version of Scotch eggs (hard-cooked eggs wrapped in sausage meat and deep-fried), soft-boiled eggs are coated with panko, fried and halved. The oozy eggs are topped with scallions and a pungent mustard sauce.

8 large eggs
1 cup all-purpose flour
1 cup panko (Japanese bread crumbs)
Canola oil, for frying
Kosher salt
Asian Mustard (below), for serving
Thinly sliced scallions and pickled onions, for garnish

1. In a medium saucepan of boiling water, simmer 6 of the eggs over moderate heat for 6 minutes. Using a slotted spoon, transfer the eggs to an ice water bath to cool. Carefully peel the eggs and transfer them to a plate.

2. In a bowl, lightly beat the remaining 2 eggs. Spread the flour and panko in 2 separate pie plates. Working with 1 shelled egg at a time, carefully dredge in the flour, then dip in the beaten egg, letting the excess drip back into the bowl. Next, dredge in the panko, gently pressing to help it adhere. Transfer the coated eggs to a plate.

3. In a large saucepan, heat 2 inches of oil to 350°. With the slotted spoon, carefully slide the coated eggs into the pan and fry, turning, until golden, 3 to 4 minutes. Transfer the eggs to paper towels to drain.

4. Cut the eggs in half lengthwise and arrange on a serving platter. Season with salt, dollop a little Asian Mustard on top and garnish. —*Johanna Ware*

ASIAN MUSTARD

In a medium bowl, whisk ¼ cup mustard powder with 3 tablespoons water and let stand for 5 minutes. Whisk in 3 tablespoons mayonnaise, 2 teaspoons each of soy sauce and rice wine vinegar and 1½ teaspoons each of sugar and olive oil. Season with kosher salt.

SMALLWARES
4605 NE Fremont St.
Portland, OR
971-229-0995
smallwarespdx.com

ACTIVE: 1 HR; TOTAL: 2 HR 45 MIN • MAKES 8 SERVINGS

SHRIMP IN BLANKETS

At Towne Food & Drink, chef Eric Hara tweaks classic pigs in blankets, using house-made lobster sausage in place of the usual hot dogs. For this less pricey version, shrimp is added to the harissa-spiced filling. It's baked in buttery puff pastry, then served warm with lobster mayonnaise.

½ pound cooked lobster meat—¼ pound finely chopped, ¼ pound cut into chunks
½ cup mayonnaise
Kosher salt and freshly ground pepper
1 pound medium shrimp, shelled and deveined
3 tablespoons minced shallot
2 tablespoons harissa
2 teaspoons finely chopped basil
2 teaspoons sweet paprika
2 garlic cloves, minced
1½ teaspoons ground fennel seeds
1 teaspoon finely chopped oregano
One 14-ounce sheet all-butter puff pastry

1. In a bowl, whisk the chopped lobster with the mayonnaise and season with salt and pepper; refrigerate.

2. In a large bowl, combine all of the remaining ingredients except the puff pastry. Season with ½ teaspoon salt and ¼ teaspoon pepper. Refrigerate the filling for 1 hour.

3. On a lightly floured work surface, roll the puff pastry into a 13-by-15-inch rectangle. Using a sharp knife, cut lengthwise into four 3¼-inch-wide strips.

4. In a food processor, pulse the filling until nearly smooth. Spoon one-fourth of the filling evenly along the bottom edge of each pastry strip. Fold the pastry over the filling to form a log; press to seal. Transfer to 2 parchment-lined baking sheets. Refrigerate until chilled, at least 30 minutes.

5. Preheat the oven to 375°. Cut each log crosswise into 10 pieces and arrange them on the baking sheets without touching. Bake for 20 to 25 minutes, shifting the pans halfway through, until the pastries are puffed and golden. Serve warm, with the lobster mayonnaise. *—Eric Hara*

TOWNE
FOOD & DRINK
705 W. Ninth St.
Los Angeles
213-623-2366
towne-la.com

TOTAL: 1 HR • MAKES 50 GYOZA

SHRIMP GYOZA

📷 PAGE 171

Lucky Belly serves these juicy dumplings with a citrus-soy dipping sauce and edamame-avocado puree. But the shrimp-and-shiitake-stuffed gyoza are delicious on their own.

¼ cup plus 1 tablespoon vegetable oil
4 ounces shiitake mushrooms, stems discarded and caps thinly sliced
4 ounces asparagus, thinly sliced crosswise
1 medium shallot, sliced
1 pound shelled and deveined shrimp
4 tablespoons oyster sauce
2 tablespoons chopped cilantro
1 scallion, finely chopped
½ teaspoon kosher salt
One 10- to 12-ounce package gyoza wrappers

1. In a skillet, heat 1 tablespoon of the oil. Stir-fry the shiitake, asparagus and shallot over high heat until softened, about 8 minutes. Transfer to a bowl to cool. In a food processor, pulse half of the shrimp until smooth. Coarsely chop the remaining shrimp. Add all of the shrimp to the asparagus with the oyster sauce, cilantro, scallion and salt.
2. Working in batches, lightly brush the edges of the gyoza wrappers with water. Spoon a scant tablespoon of the filling in the center of each wrapper and fold in half, pressing to seal. Arrange the gyoza on a wax paper–lined baking sheet, seam side up, and cover with a damp paper towel.
3. Divide the remaining ¼ cup of oil between 2 large nonstick skillets. Arrange the gyoza in the skillets seam side up in 2 concentric circles without touching. Cook over high heat until the bottoms are lightly browned, 2 minutes. Add ½ cup of water to each skillet, cover and cook until the water has evaporated and the dumplings are cooked through, about 5 minutes. Uncover the skillets and cook until the gyoza bottoms are browned and crisp, about 1 minute. Transfer the gyoza to a plate and serve.
—*Jesse Cruz*

LUCKY BELLY
50 N. Hotel St.
Honolulu
808-531-1888
luckybelly.com

TOTAL: 50 MIN • MAKES 10 CRAB CAKES

CHUNKY CRAB CAKES

Chef Bernie Kantak originally made these crab cakes for a special cocktail pairing dinner. His business partner, mixologist Richie Moe, liked them so much that he insisted Kantak add them to the regular menu.

AIOLI

- 1 roasted red bell pepper—peeled, seeded and stemmed
- 1 cup mayonnaise
- 1 garlic clove
- 1 tablespoon fresh lemon juice

Kosher salt and freshly ground pepper

CRAB CAKES

- ½ cup mayonnaise
- 1 large egg, lightly beaten
- 2 tablespoons minced red onion
- 2 tablespoons minced red bell pepper
- 1½ tablespoons fresh lemon juice
- 1 tablespoon minced jalapeño
- 2 teaspoons Dijon mustard
- 2 teaspoons Worcestershire sauce
- 1 teaspoon hot sauce
- 1 pound jumbo lump crabmeat
- ¾ cup panko, plus more for dredging
- ½ cup vegetable oil

1. MAKE THE AIOLI In a food processor, puree the roasted red pepper, mayonnaise, garlic and lemon juice. Season with salt and pepper and scrape into a bowl.

2. MAKE THE CRAB CAKES In a bowl, combine all of the ingredients except the crab, panko and oil; mix well. Gently fold in the crab and ¾ cup of panko. Scoop into ten 1-inch-thick patties, dredge in panko and transfer to a plate.

3. In a large skillet, heat ¼ cup of the oil. Fry half of the crab cakes over moderate heat until golden and cooked through, about 3 minutes per side. Transfer to paper towels to drain. Wipe out the skillet and repeat with the remaining oil and crab cakes. Serve with the aioli. *—Bernie Kantak*

CITIZEN
PUBLIC HOUSE
7111 E. Fifth Ave.
Scottsdale, AZ
480-398-4208
citizenpublichouse.com

TOTAL: 35 MIN • MAKES 4 SERVINGS

MINTY PEAS & BACON ON TOAST

Chef Gregory Vernick makes these terrific toasts by pureeing frozen peas with mint and butter, then spreading the pea butter on thick slices of sourdough bread with bacon on top. The bread soaks up the bacon fat as it toasts.

1   cup frozen peas, thawed
2   tablespoons unsalted butter, softened
2   tablespoons cream cheese, softened
¼   cup lightly packed mint leaves,
    plus chopped mint for garnish
Kosher salt
Cayenne pepper
Four ½-inch-thick slices of sourdough bread
Extra-virgin olive oil, preferably fruity,
    for brushing and garnish
12   thin bacon slices (6 ounces)

1. Preheat the oven to 400°. In a food processor, combine the peas with the butter, cream cheese and the ¼ cup of mint. Pulse until nearly smooth; season the pea butter with salt and cayenne.

2. Brush the bread with olive oil and arrange the slices on a rimmed baking sheet. Toast the bread in the oven for about 8 minutes, turning once, until lightly golden but still chewy in the center. Transfer the toasts to a work surface; leave the oven on.

3. Spread each toast with about ¼ cup of the pea butter and top with 3 slices of bacon. Arrange the toasts on the baking sheet and bake for about 10 minutes, until the bacon just starts to render. Turn on the broiler and broil the toasts 6 inches from the heat for about 3 minutes, until the bacon starts to brown. Garnish the toasts with olive oil and chopped mint and serve warm.
—Gregory Vernick

VERNICK
FOOD & DRINK
2031 Walnut St.
Philadelphia
267-639-6644
vernickphilly.com

ROYAL MONDAY
MORNING **P.166**

MINTY PEAS & BACON
ON TOAST

TOTAL: 1 HR 15 MIN PLUS 2 HR MARINATING • MAKES 8 SERVINGS

CRISPY FRIED TOFU

Bill Kim, chef at the meat-focused BellyQ, says this is a great recipe to make for people who don't like tofu. "Tell them it's cheese!" he says. "Tofu done right is delicious."

½ cup mirin
½ cup soy sauce
1½ teaspoons fresh lime juice
1½ teaspoons fresh clementine or orange juice
Two 14-ounce packages extra-firm tofu,
    drained well and cut into 8 rectangles each
3 cups rice flour, 2 large eggs, 2 cups milk
    and 2 cups panko, for breading
Vegetable oil, for frying
Kosher salt
Plum Sauce (below), for serving

1. In a baking dish, whisk the mirin, soy, lime juice, clementine juice and ¼ cup of water. Add the tofu and turn to coat. Refrigerate for 2 to 4 hours, turning once; pat dry.
2. In a shallow dish, spread 1 cup of the rice flour. In another shallow dish, whisk the eggs with the milk and the remaining 2 cups of rice flour. Spread the panko in a third shallow dish. Dredge the tofu in the flour, the egg mixture and then the panko, lightly patting the coating to help it adhere.
3. In a large saucepan, heat 1½ inches of oil to 325°. Fry the coated tofu in batches, turning, until deep golden, 7 minutes. Transfer to paper towels to drain and season with salt. Serve hot, with the Plum Sauce. —*Bill Kim*

PLUM SAUCE
In a saucepan, heat 2 tablespoons vegetable oil. Add 1 small thinly sliced onion and 2 sliced garlic cloves; cook over moderate heat, stirring, until the onion starts to brown. Add ¼ cup dark brown sugar, 5 thinly sliced black plums and 1 tablespoon tamarind paste. Cook, stirring, until soft, 12 minutes; let cool. In a blender, pulse with 1 teaspoon Sriracha until nearly smooth. Season the sauce with salt.

BELLYQ
1400 W. Randolph St.
Chicago • 312-563-1010
bellyqchicago.com

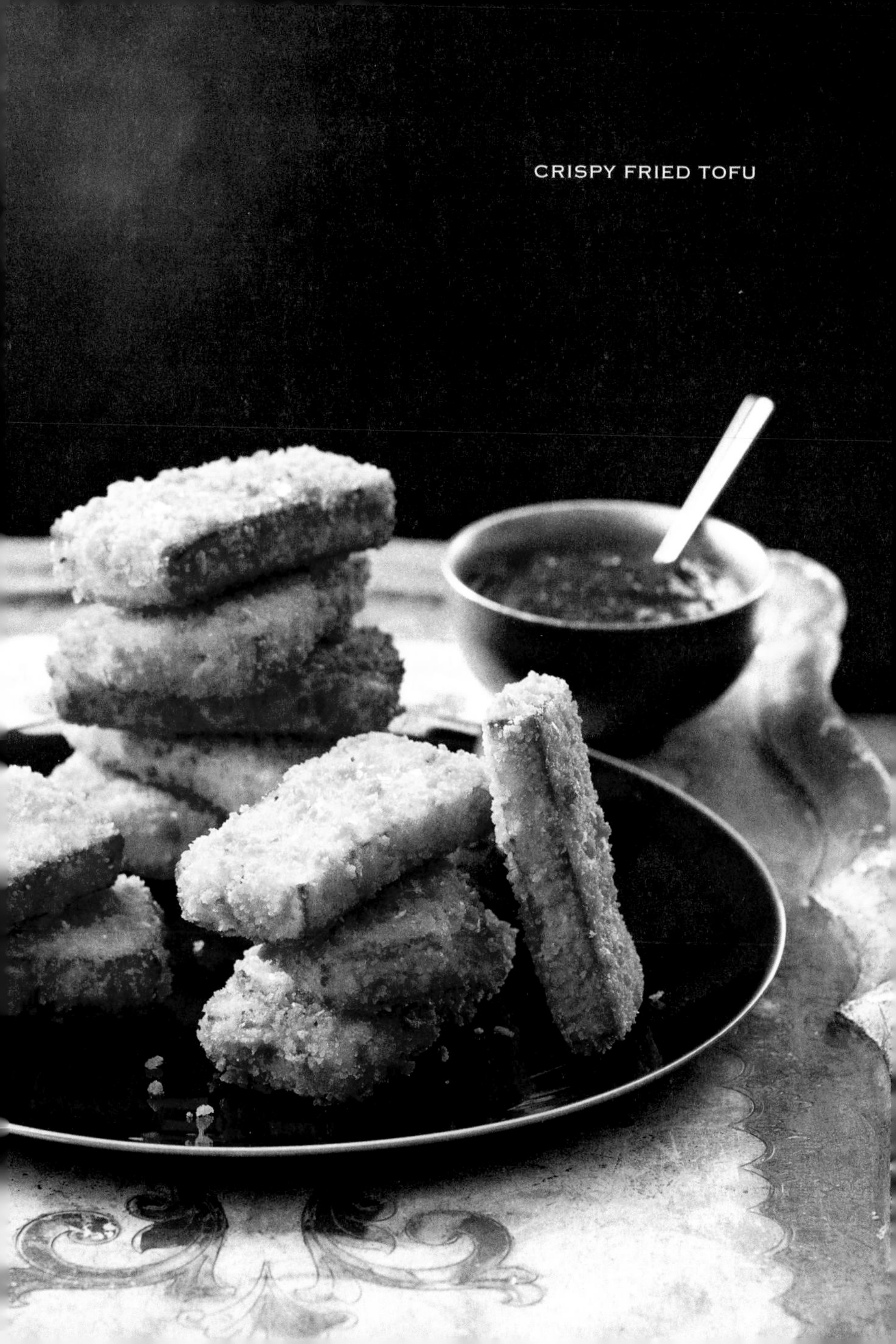

CRISPY FRIED TOFU

TOTAL: 45 MIN • MAKES 4 SERVINGS

CHICKEN WINGS WITH STOUT GLAZE

The stout glaze on these wings from Casey Lane gives them a slightly bitter, not-too-sweet flavor. They're grilled until sticky and caramelized, then sprinkled with scallion and flaxseeds.

½ cup pure maple syrup
One 12-ounce bottle stout beer
¼ cup red wine vinegar
2½ pounds chicken wings,
    tips discarded and wings split
Extra-virgin olive oil
1 tablespoon kosher salt
2 teaspoons freshly ground black pepper
1 teaspoon cayenne pepper
Flaxseeds and thinly sliced scallion, for garnish

1. In a medium saucepan, simmer the maple syrup over moderate heat until beginning to thicken slightly and darken in color, about 7 minutes. Whisk in the stout and vinegar and bring to a boil. Simmer over moderate heat, stirring occasionally, until the glaze is thickened and reduced to ¾ cup, about 12 minutes.

2. Light a grill. In a large bowl, toss the wings with olive oil and the salt, black pepper and cayenne. Grill the wings over moderately high heat, turning occasionally, until lightly charred and just cooked through, about 15 minutes.

3. Transfer the chicken wings to a large clean bowl and toss with half of the stout glaze. Return the wings to the grill and cook, turning once, just until sticky and caramelized, about 2 minutes. Return the wings to the bowl, toss with the remaining stout glaze and grill, turning once, until caramelized, 1 to 2 minutes longer. Transfer the wings to a serving platter and garnish with flaxseeds and scallion.
—*Casey Lane*

THE PARISH
840 S. Spring St.
Los Angeles
213-225-2400
theparishla.com

ACTIVE: 1 HR; TOTAL: 4 HR • MAKES 6 TO 8 SERVINGS

PORK MEATBALLS WITH TOMATO SAUCE

"I crashed and burned the first time I made these meatballs," says chef Tandy Wilson. "The sauce was way too spicy." He has since perfected the recipe. Large meatballs are great in a sub sandwich or on top of pasta; mini meatballs can be skewered with toothpicks for hors d'oeuvres.

3 cups fresh bread crumbs
1¾ cups whole milk
2½ pounds fatty ground pork
¼ cup chopped parsley
8 garlic cloves, minced
Kosher salt and freshly ground black pepper
⅓ cup extra-virgin olive oil,
plus more for greasing and drizzling
1 large onion, thinly sliced
2 teaspoons dried oregano
Two 28-ounce cans crushed tomatoes
Freshly grated Grana Padano cheese, for serving

1. In a large bowl, soak the bread crumbs in the milk for 15 minutes. Add the ground pork, parsley, half of the garlic, 1½ tablespoons of salt and 1 teaspoon of pepper; knead gently to combine. Refrigerate for 1 hour.

2. Preheat the oven to 300°. Form the meat mixture into 1½-inch balls and arrange them in a lightly oiled roasting pan. Bake for about 30 minutes, until just cooked through.

3. Meanwhile, in a saucepan, heat the ⅓ cup of oil. Add the onion, the remaining garlic and a generous pinch of salt. Cook over moderate heat until the onion is softened, 10 minutes. Add the oregano and cook until fragrant, about 2 minutes. Add the tomatoes and bring to a simmer. Cook over moderately low heat until slightly reduced, about 20 minutes. Transfer to a blender and puree until almost smooth. Season the sauce with salt and pepper.

4. Pour the sauce over the meatballs, cover tightly with foil and bake for 2 hours. Drizzle the meatballs with oil, sprinkle with cheese and serve. —*Tandy Wilson*

CITY HOUSE

1222 Fourth Ave. N.
Nashville • 615-736-5838
cityhousenashville.com

TOTAL: 1 HR • MAKES 4 TO 6 SERVINGS

FOUR-CHEESE GRILLED PESTO PIZZA

This crowd-pleasing white pizza is lightly charred on the grill and topped with a garlicky pistachio pesto and four cheeses: mozzarella, Fontina, provolone and scamorza (a cow-milk cheese that's like a dry mozzarella). If scamorza isn't available, double the amount of mozzarella.

- ½ cup unsalted roasted pistachios
- 2 small garlic cloves
- 2 cups lightly packed baby arugula
- 1 cup lightly packed basil leaves
- ½ teaspoon crushed red pepper
- ½ cup extra-virgin olive oil, plus more for brushing
- ½ cup freshly grated Parmigiano-Reggiano cheese
- Kosher salt and freshly ground black pepper
- ½ cup each of shredded mozzarella, Fontina, provolone and *scamorza* cheeses
- 1 pound pizza dough

1. In a food processor, pulse the pistachios and garlic until minced. Add the arugula, basil and crushed red pepper and pulse until minced. With the machine on, gradually add the ½ cup of oil until incorporated. Add the Parmigiano and pulse to combine. Season the pesto with salt and black pepper.

2. Light a grill or preheat a grill pan. In a bowl, toss the mozzarella with the Fontina, provolone and *scamorza*.

3. Divide the dough into 4 pieces. On a lightly floured work surface, roll or stretch each dough piece to a 10-inch oval, ⅛ inch thick. Brush the dough with oil. Grill each pizza over moderately high heat, turning once, until lightly charred on both sides and puffed, about 4 minutes. Transfer to a work surface. Spread one-fourth of the pesto on top and sprinkle with the cheeses. Season with salt and pepper.

4. Working in batches if necessary, grill the pizzas over moderately low heat, covered, until the cheese is just melted, about 5 minutes. Cut the pizzas into strips and serve hot. —*Matt Troost*

THREE ACES

1321 W. Taylor St.
Chicago · 312-243-1577
threeaceschicago.com

FOUR-CHEESE GRILLED PESTO PIZZA

Black walnut cutting board by Lostine.

TOTAL: 1 HR • MAKES 20 SLIDERS

ASIAN SLOPPY JOE SLIDERS

Food Network star Ming Tsai serves these spicy, gingery sliders at his Boston gastropub, Blue Dragon. They're based on a recipe his mother made for him when he was young: She'd fill his thermos with the ground meat and tuck the slider buns into his lunch box. "Everyone at school wanted them, so I'd usually trade a little slider for a complete lunch," says Tsai.

2 tablespoons canola oil
2 medium red onions, finely chopped
1 cup finely chopped celery
3 tablespoons *sambal oelek* or other Asian chile sauce
2½ tablespoons minced garlic
1 tablespoon minced peeled fresh ginger
Kosher salt and freshly ground pepper
1 pound ground chicken thighs
1 pound ground pork
1 cup hoisin sauce
1 cup drained canned diced tomatoes
¼ cup fresh lime juice
20 brioche dinner rolls, split and toasted
Shredded iceberg lettuce and spicy pickles (optional), for serving

1. In a large, deep skillet, heat the canola oil until shimmering. Add the onions, celery, *sambal oelek*, garlic, ginger and a generous pinch each of salt and pepper and cook over moderate heat, stirring occasionally, until the vegetables are softened, about 8 minutes. Add the ground chicken and pork and cook, stirring occasionally to break up the meat, until no pink remains, about 5 minutes. Stir in the hoisin, tomatoes and lime juice and bring to a boil. Simmer over moderately low heat, stirring occasionally, until thickened, about 20 minutes. Season the filling with salt and pepper.

2. Spoon about ¼ cup of the sloppy joe filling onto the bottom half of each roll. Top with shredded lettuce and pickles, close the sliders and serve. —*Ming Tsai*

BLUE DRAGON

324 A St. · Boston

617-338-8585

ming.com

TOTAL: 45 MIN • MAKES 6 SERVINGS

PORKY MELT SANDWICHES

These patty melts are a specialty of Top Chef contestant Dale Talde at Pork Slope. He layers juicy, cheese-filled patties, sautéed onions and pickles on marble rye, which has a hearty flavor and cool swirled pattern.

1½ pounds fatty ground pork
½ pound ground beef chuck
½ cup nonfat powdered milk
½ teaspoon freshly ground white pepper
½ teaspoon freshly grated nutmeg
½ teaspoon ground ginger
Kosher salt
1 large egg, lightly beaten
½ cup heavy cream
4 ounces sharp cheddar cheese, diced
Vegetable oil, for greasing
1 large onion, thinly sliced
Softened unsalted butter, for spreading
12 slices of marbled rye bread
Mustard and thinly sliced pickles, for serving

1. In a stand mixer fitted with the paddle, combine the ground meats, powdered milk, spices and 1 tablespoon of salt. Mix at low speed until blended. Add the egg and cream and mix until incorporated. Mix in the cheese.

2. Heat an oiled cast-iron griddle or grill pan. Shape the meat into 6 oval ½-inch-thick patties. Cook over moderate heat, turning once, until well browned and cooked through, 8 minutes. Transfer to a plate; cover loosely with foil.

3. Add the onion and a large pinch each of salt and pepper to the griddle. Cook over moderately high heat, stirring, until golden and softened, 5 minutes. Transfer to a plate.

4. Butter the bread on both sides. Griddle over moderate heat for 2 minutes, turning once. Spread with mustard. Arrange the patties on half the toasts, top with the griddled onions and pickles and serve. —*Dale Talde*

PORK SLOPE

247 Fifth Ave. • Brooklyn
718-768-7675
porkslopebrooklyn.com

ACTIVE: 45 MIN; TOTAL: 1 HR 30 MIN • MAKES 6 TO 8 SERVINGS

DORO WAT TACOS

Star chef Marcus Samuelsson fills tortillas with doro wat, *the stewed chicken dish from his native Ethiopia. It's flavored with thyme and* berbere, *a spice blend that includes chiles, allspice and ginger (available at kalustyans.com). The tacos are even tastier with a range of garnishes: chopped hard-cooked eggs, cilantro and cottage cheese, which is similar to the Ethiopian curd cheese called* aiyb.

2½ pounds skinless, boneless chicken thighs, trimmed
2 tablespoons fresh lime juice
2 teaspoons finely chopped thyme
3 tablespoons *berbere*
Kosher salt and freshly ground black pepper
4 tablespoons unsalted butter
2 large onions, thinly sliced
3 garlic cloves, minced
1 habanero chile, seeded and minced
1 tablespoon finely grated peeled fresh ginger
2 tablespoons tomato paste
½ cup red wine
1½ cups chicken stock or low-sodium broth
4 large hard-cooked eggs, finely chopped
Warm corn tortillas, for serving

1. In a bowl, rub the chicken with the lime juice, 1 teaspoon of the thyme, 1 tablespoon of the *berbere* and a generous pinch each of salt and pepper. Let stand for 30 minutes.

2. Preheat the oven to 350°. In a large, deep ovenproof skillet, melt the butter. Add the onions and cook over moderately low heat, stirring, until golden and softened, about 25 minutes. Stir in the garlic, habanero, ginger and the remaining thyme and cook until fragrant, 1 minute. Add the tomato paste and the remaining *berbere*. Cook over moderate heat until glossy, about 5 minutes. Add the wine and cook until almost evaporated, 3 minutes. Stir in the stock; bring to a boil. Add the chicken, cover and bake for 40 minutes, until tender; turn halfway through baking.

3. Shred the chicken with 2 forks. Simmer over moderately high heat until the sauce has thickened, 5 minutes. Stir in half the eggs and season with salt and pepper. Serve with tortillas and the remaining eggs. —*Marcus Samuelsson*

AMERICAN TABLE

Lincoln Center

1941 Broadway

New York City

212-671-4200

*americantablecafe
andbar.com*

TOTAL: 1 HR • MAKES 6 SERVINGS

SAUSAGES WITH GRILLED-PEPPER & MUSTARD RELISH

Sweet Italian sausages are especially good with the tangy vinaigrette here. Chef Vitaly Paley likes Nicky USA's Russian-style wild boar sausage with caraway seeds (nicky-usa.com).

1 medium red onion, sliced ½ inch thick
1½ tablespoons extra-virgin olive oil, plus more for brushing
Sea salt and freshly ground pepper
2 red bell peppers
2 poblano chiles
3 tablespoons whole-grain mustard
2 tablespoons finely chopped parsley
1½ tablespoons red wine vinegar
2 teaspoons sugar
½ teaspoon finely chopped thyme
6 sweet Italian sausages (1 pound)

1. Light a grill or preheat a grill pan. Brush the onion slices with oil and season with salt and pepper. Grill over moderate heat, turning once, until softened and lightly charred, about 3 minutes. Let cool, then coarsely chop.

2. Roast the bell peppers and poblano chiles on the grill or under a preheated broiler, turning, until charred all over. Let cool. Peel, seed and stem the peppers and chiles, then thinly slice them crosswise.

3. In a medium bowl, combine the peppers and chiles with the onion. Add the mustard, parsley, vinegar, sugar, thyme and the 1½ tablespoons of olive oil. Season the relish with salt and pepper.

4. Heat a large cast-iron skillet. Prick the sausages with a knife and cook over moderate heat, turning occasionally, until browned and cooked through, about 10 minutes. Serve with the mustard relish. —*Vitaly Paley and Ben Bettinger*

IMPERIAL
410 SW Broadway
Portland, OR
503-228-7222
imperialpdx.com

TOTAL: 45 MIN • MAKES 6 SERVINGS

THE HAVEN BURGER

The Haven Burger from Greg Daniels is topped with a supremely satisfying mix of creamy, salty blue cheese, tangy pickled onions, sweet roasted red pepper slices and crisp arugula.

1 cup mayonnaise
1 garlic clove, minced
Kosher salt and freshly ground black pepper
Cayenne pepper
2 pounds ground beef chuck
Vegetable oil or canola oil, for brushing
6 ounces mild blue cheese, such as Saint Agur, crumbled
6 brioche hamburger buns, split and toasted
¼ cup plus 2 tablespoons chopped jarred pickled onions
1 cup lightly packed baby arugula
2 roasted red bell peppers—peeled, stemmed, seeded and thinly sliced

1. In a bowl, whisk the mayonnaise with the garlic and season with salt, black pepper and cayenne.

2. Heat a cast-iron griddle or grill pan. Shape the ground meat into six ½-inch-thick patties. Brush the burgers with oil and season generously with salt and black pepper. Cook the burgers over moderately high heat until they are well browned on the bottom, about 4 minutes. Flip the burgers and cook for 2 minutes longer. Top each burger with some of the blue cheese, tent with foil and cook for 2 minutes longer, until the cheese is slightly melted and the burgers are medium-rare.

3. Spread the buns with the garlic mayo. Set the burgers on the buns and top with the pickled onions, arugula and roasted pepper slices. Close the burgers and serve right away. *—Greg Daniels*

BURGER HAVEN AT HAVEN GASTROPUB
42 S. De Lacey Ave.
Pasadena, CA
626-768-9555
havengastropub.com

DRINK. WELL.
IN AUSTIN, P.209

TOP 100 NEW AMERICAN BARS

F&W COCKTAILS DEPUTY EDITOR JIM MEEHAN OF PDT IN NEW YORK CITY COMPILED THIS LIST OF THE COUNTRY'S BEST NEW BARS, MANY RUN BY MIXOLOGISTS FEATURED IN THIS BOOK.

EAST COAST

Boston

BRICK & MORTAR
Located above Central Kitchen restaurant, this industrial-cool space features exposed brick, a copper bar and innovative cocktails like the Sentimental Gentleman, made with Scotch and walnut liqueur. *567 Massachusetts Ave.; 617-491-0016; brickandmortarbar.com.*

THE HAWTHORNE
The newest project from star mixologist Jackson Cannon and restaurateur Garrett Harker (of the adjoining Eastern Standard and Island Creek Oyster Bar) has the feel of an intimate living room. *500A Commonwealth Ave.; 617-532-9150; thehawthornebar.com.*

New York City

ATTABOY
Elite bartenders Sam Ross and Michael McIlroy are behind the bar at this little Lower East Side cocktail joint in the former Milk & Honey space. *134 Eldridge St., Manhattan; no phone.*

BOOKER & DAX
This high-tech cocktail bar next to Momofuku Ssäm Bar is headed by mad scientist–mixologist Dave Arnold, who creates modernist drinks like a Gin and Juice made with clarified grape juice. *207 Second Ave., Manhattan; 212-254-3500; momofuku.com.*

THE DAILY
This high-end NoLita cocktail lounge has an old gentlemen's-club atmosphere and food and drink specials that change every day. *210 Elizabeth St., Manhattan; 212-343-7011; thedaily-nyc.com.*

THE DEAD RABBIT GROCERY & GROG
UK bartenders Sean Muldoon and Jack McGarry (**P. 108**) created this saloon with a nod to old New York. The taproom offers whiskeys and beer; the upstairs parlor serves over 70 historically accurate classic cocktails. *30 Water St., Manhattan; 646-422-7906; deadrabbitnyc.com.*

DONNA
Leif Huckman opened this Central American–themed South Williamsburg parlor featuring original cocktails like the Morgan Town, made with bourbon, Ramazzotti amaro, Dolin blanc vermouth and mole bitters. *27 Broadway, Brooklyn; 646-568-6622; donnabklyn.com.*

EXPERIMENTAL COCKTAIL CLUB
Frenchmen Romée de Goriainoff, Olivier Bon and Pierre-Charles Cros are at the helm of this outpost of the Paris-based Experimental Cocktail Club. *191 Chrystie St., Manhattan; no phone; experimentalcocktailclubny.com.*

EXTRA FANCY
This upscale clam shack and bar in Williamsburg serves craft beers, ciders, wines by the glass and cocktails like the Willy Bee: Campari, Cinzano bianco, lemon, watermelon and tonic water. *302 Metropolitan Ave., Brooklyn; 347-422-0939; extrafancybklyn.com.*

Top 100 New American Bars

New York City CONTINUED

THE IDES
Located on the rooftop of Williamsburg's Wythe Hotel, Andrew Tarlow's hip terrace bar features craft cocktails and sweeping views of the Manhattan skyline. *Wythe Hotel, 80 Wythe Ave., Brooklyn; 718-460-8000; wythehotel.com.*

THE NOMAD HOTEL
Eleven Madison Park's Leo Robitschek (**P.82**) is behind the 24-foot-long mahogany bar at The NoMad. The hotel's ornate two-level library also transforms into a cocktail lounge by night. *1170 Broadway, Manhattan; 212-796-1500; thenomadhotel.com.*

POURING RIBBONS
This is the newest project from the Alchemy Consulting team, including Joaquín Simó (**P. 146**) and Troy Sidle (**P. 148**). Cocktails are arranged in an innovative matrix and measured by two scales: "refreshing to spirituous" and "comforting to adventurous." *225 Avenue B, Manhattan; 917-656-6788; pouringribbons.com.*

THE SHANTY
This friendly bar connected to the New York Distilling Company makes cocktails using the gin distilled next door and has local beers on tap. *79 Richardson St., Brooklyn; 718-878-3579; nydistilling.com.*

Philadelphia

1 TIPPLING PLACE
A rotating list of barrel-aged cocktails and seasonal punches anchors the menu at this cozy mid-20th-century-style parlor. *2006 Chestnut St.; 215-665-0456; 1tpl.com.*

EMMANUELLE
This intimate, candlelit space located in the back of the open-air Piazza at Schmidt's creates serious craft cocktails, including the absinthe-loaded Death in the Afternoon. *N. Hancock St. and Germantown Ave.; 215-791-8090.*

HOP SING LAUNDROMAT
Led by an eccentric barman-proprietor known only as Lêe, this speakeasy has strict house rules: no cell phones and no photos. Concoctions include the Henry "Box" Brown, made with fresh red grape juice and aged rum. *1029 Race St.; no phone; hopsinglaundromat.com.*

LEMON HILL
Named for a nearby historic Federal-style mansion, this gastropub offers small plates, entrées and seasonal cocktails made with house tinctures like blueberry-rooibos syrup and dandelion bitters. *747 N. 25th St.; 215-232-2299; lemonhillphilly.com.*

VERNICK FOOD & DRINK
Chef Greg Vernick's neighborhood restaurant features a small but comprehensive dinner menu and food-friendly cocktails like the Red Charlotte (vodka, Pinot Noir reduction, allspice, citrus juices and sparkling wine). *2031 Walnut St.; 267-639-6644; vernickphilly.com.*

Washington, DC area

THE EDDY BAR
Capitol Hill's alchemy expert Gina Chersevani is behind the bar at this nautical-inspired 20-seat spot inside Hank's Oyster Bar. *Hank's Oyster Bar, 633 Pennsylvania Ave. SE, Washington, DC; 202-733-1971; hanksoysterbar.com.*

HOGO
Tom Brown (also of the Passenger restaurant and bar next door) opened this rum-focused establishment to serve inventive tiki drinks and house punches. *1017 Seventh St. NW, Washington, DC; 202-393-1313; hogodc.com.*

RANGE
This restaurant-bar complex from Bryan Voltaggio creates wild house syrups and infusions. Their "beef ice," made from veal consommé, is used in the Vegan Sacrifice cocktail (Scotch, ginger and cayenne). *5335 Wisconsin Ave. NW, Washington, DC; 202-803-8020; voltrange.com.*

THE SHANTY
IN NEW YORK CITY

Top 100 New American Bars

Washington, DC area CONTINUED

ROOM 11
This corner bar and restaurant in Columbia Heights offers an extensive wine list and a cocktail program focused on amari, aperitifs and digestifs. *3234 11th St. NW, Washington, DC; 202-332-3234; room11dc.com.*

SOCIETY FAIR
The wine-influenced cocktail list at the bar here is by famed local mixologist Todd Thrasher (also of PX and TNT). *277 S. Washington St., Alexandria, VA; 703-683-3247; societyfair.net.*

TNT
Tucked into the back of Eamonn's restaurant, TNT features graffiti on the walls, hard rock on the stereo and creative drinks like the Cocktail Left on the Nightstand (smoked whiskey and flat Coke). *2413 Columbia Pike, Arlington, VA; 703-920-0315; eamonnsdublinchipper.com.*

GREAT LAKES AND MIDWEST

Chicago

THE BARRELHOUSE FLAT
The Violet Hour alum Stephen Cole (**P. 112**) creates classics-inspired cocktails and books live ragtime acts on weekends. *2624 N. Lincoln Ave., 773-857-0421; barrelhouseflat.com.*

BILLY SUNDAY
At this old-school tavern, chef Matthias Merges of Yusho serves original drinks like Against the Bliss, made with New Western gin, rhubarb sherbet, lemon and rose bitters. *3143 W. Logan Blvd.; 773-661-2485; billy-sunday.com.*

BUB CITY
Part BBQ restaurant and part Americana-themed bar, Bub City features live country music and whiskey-focused cocktails. *435 N. Clark St.; 312-610-4200; bubcitychicago.com.*

SCOFFLAW
This speakeasy-style parlor specializes in gin cocktails; mixologist and owner Danny Shapiro, formerly of the Whistler, is at the helm. *3201 W. Armitage Ave.; 773-252-9700; scofflawchicago.com.*

THREE DOTS & A DASH
Named after a 1940s rum drink and also Morse code for "V" as in "victory," this tiki-style bar from Paul McGee (**P. 92**) and the Melman brothers is right below sister establishment Bub City. *435 N. Clark St.; no phone; threedotschicago.com.*

TRENCHERMEN
Veteran mixologist Tona Palomino (formerly of NYC's WD-50) serves creative drinks like the Green Hornet, a gin-and-tonic riff made with celery juice and bitters, to pair with bar snacks like pickle tater tots. *2039 W. North Ave.; 773-661-1540; trenchermen.com.*

YUSHO
The bar menu at this yakitori-inspired restaurant has a wide selection of sake and cocktails like the Undertone (rye whiskey, amaro, lemon and Szechwan peppercorn bitters). *2853 N. Kedzie Ave.; 773-904-8558; yusho-chicago.com.*

Wisconsin

BRAISE
With an entire wall made from reclaimed barn boards, the cozy interior of Braise echoes the restaurant's farm-to-table philosophy. The cocktail list is based on seasonal infusions, including a toasted nut–enhanced rye whiskey used in their Sazerac. *1101 S. Second St., Milwaukee; 414-212-8843; braiselocalfood.com.*

FOREQUARTER
The bar program here highlights small, regional and domestic spirits and focuses on aperitifs and digestifs. The cardamom-and-chile-infused Apple Pipe is made with a mixture of apple brandy, mezcal and dry vermouth. *708¼ E. Johnson St., Madison; 608-609-4717; under groundfoodcollective.org.*

LUCKY JOE'S TIKI ROOM
This tropical-themed bar and lounge specializes in wacky riffs on classic tiki cocktails, like a peach pie–flavored mai tai. *196 S. Second St., Milwaukee; 414-271-8454;* luckyjoestiki.com.

Minneapolis

CAFÉ MAUDE AT LORING PARK
This bar and bistro concocts inventive cocktails like the Madhatteran: High West Double Rye, amaro, Punt e Mes, maraschino liqueur and orange bitters. Small plates and drink specials are served during their famous daily "leisure hour," which starts at 5 p.m. *1612 Harmon Pl.; 612-767-9080;* cafemaude.com.

EAT STREET SOCIAL
Ira Koplowitz and Nicholas Kosevich (**P.32**), founders of Bittercube artisanal bitters, create drinks like Of the Older Fashioned using a trio of their own bitters: Cherry Bark Vanilla, Orange and Bolivar. *18 W. 26th St.; 612-767-6850;* eatstreetsocial.com.

Missouri

BASSO
Located below the Restaurant at The Cheshire, this subterranean gastropub serves wood-oven pizzas and Italian spirit–based cocktails like the Fernet Abouddit: Fernet-Branca, maple rye, sweet vermouth, lemon juice and cherry bitters. *7036 Clayton Ave., St. Louis; 314-932-7820;* basso-stl.com.

HENDRICKS BBQ
This BBQ joint has a bar in the basement that features whiskey and house-distilled moonshine cocktails along with live blues music. *1200 S. Main St., St. Charles; 636-724-8600;* hendricksbbq.com.

THE KILL DEVIL CLUB
Bartender-restaurateur Ryan Maybee consulted on the opening of this "adult oasis" that specializes in live jazz and punches. *31 E. 14th St., Kansas City; 816-588-1132;* killdevilclub.com.

PORT FONDA
What started as a Mexican food truck is now a restaurant and bar with an extensive list of tequilas and mezcals. *4141 Pennsylvania Ave., Kansas City; 816-216-6462;* portfondakc.com.

SOUTH

Louisville

MEAT
The menu at Meat is designed for carnivorous drinkers: Cocktails are described as well-done, medium and rare, based on stiffness and complexity. *1076 E. Washington St.; 502-354-3212;* meatinlouisville.com.

THE SILVER DOLLAR
This bar and restaurant is inspired by two things: Bakersfield-style country music and Kentucky straight bourbon whiskey. *1761 Frankfort Ave.; 502-259-9540;* whiskeybythedrink.com.

ST. CHARLES EXCHANGE
With its sleek leather barstools, crystal chandeliers and pre-Prohibition cocktail menu, this restaurant and lounge exudes the feel of an early 1900s hotel lobby bar. *113 S. Seventh St.; 502-618-1917;* stcharlesexchange.com.

Nashville

ROLF & DAUGHTERS
This restaurant offers a Southern ingredient–driven take on Italian peasant food and drinks like the rum-based Sorghum Swizzle. *700 Taylor St.; 615-866-9897;* rolfanddaughters.com.

Atlanta area

PAPER PLANE
Mixologist Paul Calvert (formerly of Pura Vida and the Sound Table) is behind this smart, sexy restaurant-bar on the outskirts of Atlanta. *340 Church St., Decatur, GA;* paperplaneatlanta.com.

Top 100 New American Bars

Atlanta area CONTINUED

SEVEN LAMPS
With the Crunch Punch, featuring Peanut Butter Cap'n Crunch–infused rye whiskey, you can drink your dessert at this sleek, open kitchen and bar. *3400 Around Lenox Rd. No. 217, Atlanta; 404-467-8950;* sevenlampsatl.com.

Charleston, South Carolina

THE ORDINARY
The drinks menu at chef Mike Lata's oyster bar is tightly focused, offering just a handful of carefully crafted cocktails at a time. *544 King St.; 843-414-7060;* eattheordinary.com.

PROOF
This bar features a rotating menu of chalkboard specials (duck rillettes, sloppy joes) and sophisticated cocktails like a Dark and Stormy made with house ginger beer. *437 King St.; 843-793-1422;* facebook.com/proofcharleston.

Miami & Miami Beach

BLACKBIRD ORDINARY
The funky cocktails here are named after birds. The Egret, an off-the-menu special, is a mix of mint, sugar, lime, apple cider and gin. *729 SW First Ave., Miami; 305-671-3307;* blackbirdordinary.com.

THE BROKEN SHAKER
This poolside lounge at the newly renovated Freehand Miami hostel serves refreshing cocktails made with homemade syrups and garden herbs from the creative mixology duo Gabriel Orta and Elad Zvi (**P. 101**). *Freehand Miami, 2727 Indian Creek Dr., Miami Beach; 305-531-2727;* thefreehand.com.

LANTAO
This restaurant and lounge explores the flavors of Southeast Asian street food. The Hidden Gun cocktail, for example, features Thai chile–infused vodka. *1717 Collins Ave., Miami Beach; 305-604-1800;* lantaorestaurant.com.

THE REGENT COCKTAIL CLUB
With wood accents, cocktails served neat and a cigar-friendly patio, this retro lounge harks back to the hotel's opening in 1941. *Gale South Beach & Regent Hotel, 1690 Collins Ave., Miami Beach; 305-673-0199;* galehotel.com.

New Orleans

BELLOCQ
Neal Bodenheimer, Kirk Estopinal (**P. 154**) and Matthew Kohnke of Cure brought their mixology expertise to the cobbler-and-punch-based cocktail menu at this hotel lounge. *The Hotel Modern, 936 St. Charles Ave.; 504-962-0911;* thehotelmodern.com.

SOBOU
Creole street food is king at this restaurant south of Bourbon Street, where they serve "Two Bit" 25-cent martinis during lunch. Abigail Gullo (formerly of NYC's Fort Defiance and The Beagle) is the head bar chef. *310 Chartres St.; 504-552-4095;* sobounola.com.

Houston

THE BAD NEWS BAR
The newest project from Justin Burrow (formerly of Anvil Bar & Refuge), this straightforward second-floor bar has $2 Lone Star beers, specialty frozen blended cocktails and a laid-back attitude. *308 Main St.; no phone or website yet.*

JULEP
Alba Huerta, former general manager of Anvil Bar & Refuge, opened this bar and restaurant in a historic former uniform factory with the help of Houston mixologist Bobby Heugel (**P. 72**). *1919 Washington Ave.;* facebook.com/julepHOU.

THE PASS & PROVISIONS
Provisions, a casual bar and dining area housed in the same historic warehouse as The Pass restaurant, offers drinks like Edison's Lighthouse (rum, genever, Pineau des Charentes and rosemary) alongside small plates and pizzas. *807 Taft St.; 713-628-9020;* passandprovisions.com.

Austin

DRINK.WELL.

This pub in the city's North Loop offers craft beers, wines and drinks arranged into categories like "Sour Patch Kids," tart, citrus-forward, shaken cocktails; and "Dark & Lovely," drinks that are boozy, bitter and bracing. *207 E. 53rd St.; 512-614-6683;* drinkwellaustin.com.

MIDNIGHT COWBOY

Located in a former brothel behind an unmarked door, this reservations-only lounge from Alamo Drafthouse beverage director Bill Norris (**P.118**) focuses on tableside cocktail presentations to encourage customer interaction. *313 E. Sixth St.; 512-843-2715;* midnightcowboymodeling.com.

WEATHER UP

This sister location of mixologist-mogul Kathryn Weatherup's New York City bar group serves over 100 custom beverages divided into six categories based on the type of preparation: on the rock; shaken up; tall and cool; stirred up; served long; and fizzes, flips and sours. *1808 E. Cesar Chavez St.; 512-524-0464.*

Dallas

BOULEVARDIER

Named after the classic bourbon-based cocktail, this French bistro is located in the Bishop Arts District. In addition to classic cocktails, the drinks list includes specialty creations like Smash de la Saison: rye whiskey poured over shaved ice and garnished with fruit and mint. *408 N. Bishop Ave. #108; 214-942-1828;* dallasboulevardier.com.

CENTRAL 214

Jacques Bezuidenhout of San Francisco's Harry Denton's Starlight Room is behind the beverage program here. He infuses regional ingredients from jams to local greens into refreshing cocktails. The First Course, for instance, includes gin, arugula, lime and Texas honey. *5680 N. Central Expressway; 214-443-9339;* central214.com.

THE ESTABLISHMENT

This intimate reservations-required spot is a new take on a traditional canteen-and-oyster-bar. There are no servers or cocktail menus—only a list of spirits. To order drinks, patrons have a conversation with the bartenders. *4513 Travis St.; 214-928-7700;* facebook.com/theestablishmentdallas.

SOUTHWEST

Arizona

BAR CRUDO

To pair with the Italian-style raw dishes served at Bar Crudo's daily happy hour, mixologist-sommelier Micah Olson mixes drinks like the Dazed and Infused: strawberry-spiked Aperol, passion fruit syrup, lime and sparkling wine. *3603 E. Indian School Rd., Phoenix; 602-358-8666;* crudoaz.com.

BLUE HOUND KITCHEN & COCKTAILS

The friendly gastropub menu here includes shareable plates to accompany Blue Hound's classic and reinvented cocktails and thoughtful mocktails. There's also a special vermouth program headed by main barkeep Shel Bourdon. *2 E. Jefferson St., Phoenix; 602-258-0231;* bluehoundkitchen.com.

PENCA

Inspired by owner Patricia Schwabe's Mexico City roots, Penca offers authentic dishes like poblano chile rellenos and agave-based cocktails from bar manager Luke Anable. *50 East Broadway, Tucson; no phone;* facebook.com/pencatucson.

SAINT HOUSE

Both the food and cocktails are influenced by the Caribbean islands and other rum-producing regions at this latest project from local restaurateurs Travis Reese and Nicole Flowers. *256 E. Congress St., Tucson; no phone.*

Top 100 New American Bars

Arizona CONTINUED

WINDSOR
This neighborhood restaurant features an elaborate DIY Bloody Mary bar during weekend brunch along with house cocktails. The No. 06, for instance, includes gin, strawberry syrup and apple cider vinegar. *5223 N. Central Ave., Phoenix; 602-279-1111; windsoraz.com.*

Las Vegas

CULINARY DROPOUT
Located in the Hard Rock Hotel & Casino, this bar has a relaxed vibe, live music and cocktails like the signature After School Special, made with raspberry tea–infused tequila. *4455 Paradise Rd.; 702-522-8100; hardrockhotel.com.*

WEST COAST

San Diego

THE LION'S SHARE
At this gastropub, game-focused bar food like port-glazed antelope ribs accompanies drinks like Monks Gone Wild: strawberry-infused Pimm's and green Chartreuse. *629 Kettner Blvd.; 619-564-6924; lionssharesd.com.*

POLITE PROVISIONS
Mixologist Erick Castro (P.56) is behind the bar program at this reinvention of a 1950s American drugstore hangout. Beer, craft soda and house-made cocktails flow from over 30 different taps. *4693 30th St.; politeprovisions.com.*

Los Angeles

BESTIA
This bar and restaurant in downtown L.A.'s Arts District serves modern Italian takes on classic cocktails from mixologist Julian Cox (P.76), like a Brandy Crusta with Amaro Nonino. *2121 Seventh Pl.; 213-514-5724; bestiala.com.*

HOTEL JUNIPER
The Houston brothers' (Harvard & Stone, Pour Vous) newest project has a hidden entrance, a gift shop selling candy and nostalgic items and 12 of L.A.'s most talented mixologists behind the bar. The menu is gin- and whiskey-forward. *1727 N. Hudson Ave.; 323-465-1902.*

THE PARISH
Mixologist John Coltharp whips up inventive drinks like the Disco Nap—grappa, Aperol, lemon and mint—at chef Casey Lane's tribute to the English gastropub. *840 S. Spring St.; 213-225-2400; theparishla.com.*

POUR VOUS
The sumptuous drinks menu at this Parisian-themed lounge is divided into sections such as Parfum, Potion and Santé. The dress code encourages "cocktail attire," i.e., no baseball caps or flip-flops. *5574 Melrose Ave.; 323-871-8699; pourvousla.com.*

SASSAFRAS
Inspired by the hospitality and charm of the South, Sassafras was constructed from a Savannah town house that was disassembled and relocated to Hollywood. *1233 N. Vine St.; 323-467-2800; sassafrassaloon.com.*

San Francisco area

LOLINDA
From the team behind Delaros and Beretta, this Argentinean-style steak house serves refreshing cocktails like the Gilda (Calle 23 blanco tequila, lime, pineapple and cinnamon) alongside empanadas, ceviches and blood sausage. *2518 Mission St., San Francisco; 415-550-6970; lolindasf.com.*

PRIZEFIGHTER
The straightforward, no-nonsense menu here features specialty punch bowls like Mary Rockett's Milk Punch (brandy, lemon and nutmeg) along with house-made soda-fountain cocktails from Jon Santer (P.95). *6702 Hollis St., Emeryville, CA; no phone; prizefighterbar.com.*

POUR VOUS
IN LOS ANGELES

San Francisco area CONTINUED

RICH TABLE

Cocktails like the Dutch Windmill—rum, spiced blood orange, lime and honey—exemplify the local, market-fresh philosophy at Evan and Sarah Rich's restaurant. *199 Gough St., San Francisco; 415-355-9085; richtablesf.com.*

TRADITION

This bar from the team behind Bourbon & Branch features vintage American liquor ads and nine "snugs," private booths that were used to seat women in 19th-century pubs. *441 Jones St., San Francisco; 415-474-2284; tradbar.com.*

TRICK DOG

Inspired by the Pantone guide, Trick Dog offers a color wheel–themed cocktail menu. The white-hued Polar Bear, for instance, is made with mezcal, Dolin blanc and crème de menthe. *3010 20th St., San Francisco; 415-471-2999; trickdogbar.com.*

Napa Valley

GOOSE & GANDER

Scott Beatie pairs elegant libations like the Bali spice–infused old-fashioned with chef Kelly McCown's rustic bar food. *1245 Spring St., St. Helena; 707-967-8779; goosegander.com.*

THE THOMAS

Renowned mixologists Naren Young and Linden Pride head up the beverage program at Fagiani's Bar at The Thomas. They use house-made ingredients like jasmine-citrus bitters and fresh bell pepper juice. *813 Main St., Napa; 707-226-7821; thethomas-napa.com.*

Portland, Oregon

AVA GENE'S

Barman Evan Zimmerman's carefully curated cocktail list has just eight drinks meant to showcase Italian *aperitivos* and *digestivos* like Cynar and grappa. *3377 SE Division St.; 971-229-0571; avagenes.com.*

IMPERIAL / PENNY DINER

Mixologist Brandon Wise adds clever culinary twists to drinks, incorporating ingredients like hickory chip–infused vermouth in his riff on the Manhattan. There are also two regularly rotating cocktails served on tap. *410 SW Broadway; 503-228-7222; imperialpdx.com.*

KASK

This funky saloon next to Grüner Restaurant features a changing selection of small plates, punches and cocktails like Bicycles and Baskets (rye, Aperol, St-Germain elderflower liqueur and lemon). *1215 SW Adler St.; 503-241-7163.*

LUC LAC

Named for the Vietnamese phrase meaning "shaking" or "in movement," Luc Lac boasts an impressive list of both boozy and nonalcoholic options. The Ca Phe Cola includes house-carbonated Vietnamese coffee, smoked salt and orange zest. *835 SW Second Ave.; 503-222-0047; luclackitchen.com.*

RADAR

This European *futbol*-centric sports bar serves small plates like pork and cotija grits from an open kitchen along with cocktails like the Radar Standard, mixed with gin and house-made tonic water. *3951 N. Mississippi Ave.; 503-841-6948; radarpdx.com.*

RAVEN & ROSE

Inspired by the 1883 building that houses Raven & Rose, bar director Dave Shenaut's concoctions are complex and Victorian-themed. Rotating $4 punches and $2 to $6 small plates like fried cauliflower with pickle sauce are served during their daily happy hour. *1331 SW Broadway; 503-222-7673; ravenandrosepdx.com.*

THE WOODSMAN TAVERN

In addition to the list of smoked charcuterie, the menu at Duane Sorenson's tavern includes 14 rotating taps and specialty cocktails. The Cut Tooth is made with rum, Heering cherry liqueur, Ramazzotti amaro and lime juice. *4537 SE Division St.; 971-373-8264; woodsmantavern.com.*

Seattle area

CANON
This whiskey and bitters emporium offers menu items like Angostura-Bourbon Nuts and a Smoking Monkey cocktail made with banana-infused Jameson Irish whiskey. *928 12th Ave., Seattle; 206-552-9755; canonseattle.com.*

CLOVER
Self-proclaimed liquor geek Kristi Gamble describes the cocktails on Clover's comprehensive menu as crisp, exuberant, effervescent or current. The crisp gin-based Satan's Whiskers includes both sweet and dry vermouth, orange juice and bitters. *911 E. Sharp Ave., Spokane, WA; 509-487-2937; cloverspokane.com.*

VESSEL
The cocktail offerings change constantly at this sleek, industrial-feeling bar that boasts a staff of 25 rotating bartenders. A recent example is the Cognac-based Zeus' Wrath made with Gosling's rum, lime, honey and Greek yogurt. *624 Olive Way, Seattle; 206-623-3325; vesselseattle.com.*

MOUNTAIN

Colorado

ACE
Patrons can share Asian-influenced plates like Chinese barbecue–glazed ribs along with scorpion bowls, sake and house cocktails between games at this ping-pong hall. *501 E. 17th Ave., Denver; 303-800-7705; acedenver.com.*

BRAMBLE & HARE
From the restaurateurs behind Black Cat Farm Table Bistro, this farmhouse kitchen and pub serves homey late-night snacks with their simple, rustic cocktails. After 11 p.m., all listed cocktails are $5. *1970 13th St., Boulder; 303-444-9110; brambleandhare.com.*

JUSTICE SNOW'S
This early 1900s–inspired restaurant and bar inside the historic Wheeler Opera House has a comprehensive craft-cocktail list including tableside punch bowls and traditional absinthe fountains. Joshua Smith, formerly of TAG and Williams & Graham, is behind the bar. *Wheeler Opera House, 328 E. Hyman Ave., Aspen; 970-429-8192; justicesnows.com.*

LINGER
Formerly a mortuary, this slightly macabre bar and restaurant features small plates and cocktails like the Devil Inside, made with rye whiskey, Cynar, The Velvet Devil Merlot and lemon. *2030 W. 30th Ave., Denver; 303-993-3120; lingerdenver.com.*

THE SQUEAKY BEAN
The quirky drinks menu here is based on popular '80s flicks. The "Weird Science" section includes drinks with experimental preparations; the "Rocky III" cocktails are served over hand-cut ice cubes. *1500 Wynkoop St. #101, Denver; 303-623-2665; thesqueakybean.net.*

WILLIAMS & GRAHAM
Guests pass through a door disguised as a bookcase to reach barman Sean Kenyon's (**P.98**) speakeasy-style cocktail haven. Kenyon's signature drinks include the Blackberry Sage Smash: fresh blackberries, sage and Williams & Graham Select Single Barrel Knob Creek bourbon, bottled from barrels specially chosen by Kenyon. *3160 Tejon St., Denver; 303-997-8886; williamsandgraham.com.*

Jackson Hole, Wyoming

THE ROSE
This plush, old-fashioned lounge in the Pink Garter Theatre features elegant cocktails like the Ten Cent Claude, made with bourbon, Darjeeling tea syrup and muddled citrus. *50 W. Broadway; 307-733-1500; therosejh.com.*

THE TEMPEST **P.98**

RECIPE INDEX

PAGE NUMBERS IN **BOLD** INDICATE PHOTOGRAPHS.

Recipe Index

Recipe Index

BARWARE GUIDE

GLASSWARE

P.8 [1] *"I Professionali"* martini glass by Colle, tableartonline.com; [2] *"Madrid"* glass by LSA International, elementsforhome.com; [3] *"Carat"* glass by Lena Bergström, orrefors.us; [4] *"Basso"* wineglass, calvinklein.com; [5] *"Wave"* highball glass by Donna Karan, lenox.com; [6] *"Patrician"* Champagne cup by Josef Hoffmann for Lobmeyr, neuegalerie.org; [7] *"Simple"* pilsner glass by Deborah Ehrlich for Moss, mossonline.com; [9] *"Simple"* flute, nouvelstudio.com; [10] *"Slightly Different"* fizz glass by Deborah Ehrlich, erbutler.com; *"Sussex"* wallpaper from Designers Guild, designersguild.com.

HOME BAR TOOLS

P.10 [1] *"Diamond"* ice pick, [4] *premium julep strainer*, [6] *"AG" cobbler shaker*, [8] *"Baron" strainer* and [11] *"Yarai" mixing glass*, cocktail kingdom.com; [2] *bar spoon*, caskstore.com; [5] *"Chef Sommelier" corkscrew* by L'Atelier du Vin, fitzsu.com; [7] *martini atomizer*, winestuff.com; [9] *citrus press* by Norpro, amazon.com; [10] *Boston shaker* and [12] *cocktail measure*, alessishop.com; [13] *grater*, us.microplane.com; [14] *PUG! muddler* by Chris Gallagher from Mjölk, wnjones.com/pug; [15] *strainer*, rosleusa.com.

ESSENTIAL SPIRITS

P.12 [Aperitifs, Spirit-Based] *"Alexis" glass* by Theresienthal; **P.13** [Absinthe] *"Tissage" glass* by Paola Navone for Egizia from TableArt; [Vodka] *"Chandi" glass* by Paola Navone for Egizia from TableArt; [Gin] *"Palatin" glass* by Theresienthal from TableArt. **P.14** [Tequila] *"Mami" glass* by Alessi from Fitzsu; [Rum] *"Otto" glass* by Theresienthal; [Whiskey] *"Samira" glass* by Theresienthal; [Brandy] *"Newport" glass* by Theresienthal; [Amari] *"Source" glass* by Hering Berlin from TableArt; [Liqueurs] *"Gigi" glass* by Arnolfo di Cambio from Fitzsu.

APERITIFS

P.25 *"Stone Collection"* whiskey glasses by Jiči Pelcl, unicahome.com. **P.27** *"Claire"* goblet, williamyeowardcrystal.com. **P.33** *"Cascade"* tumbler by Sugahara, dandelionsf.com. **P.37** *"Variations"* glasses by Patricia Urquiola for Baccarat.

VODKA

P.38 Glass bowl from The End of History, 212-647-7598; cocktail picks and jigger, cocktail kingdom.com; *"Chandernagor"* glass by Hermès, wealthytables.com. **P.41** *"Club Stirrer"* swizzle stick by Ciovere, 401-864-4377; *"Crocodile"* wallpaper, brettdesignwallpaper.com. **P.43** *"Square"* tall glass by Sugahara, dandelionsf.com; glass from The End of History, 212-647-7598. **P.47** *"Cliff"* glass by Nason Moretti, table artonline.com; Sieger by Furstenberg *"Sip of Gold"* Champagne cup, fitzsu.com. **P.49** *"Gigolo"* wineglass by Nason Moretti, tableartonline.com. **P.53** *"Frosted Dot"* coupes, bhldn.com; *"Celeste"* cocktail shaker, ralphlaurenhome.com.

GIN

P.54 *"Manhattan"* ice bucket and highball glasses by Rogaska, bloomingdales.com; *"Montgomery"* jigger, ralphlaurenhome.com. **P.57** *"Relax"* glasses by Sugahara, dandelionsf.com. **P.61** *"Newport"* glass by Theresienthal, tableartonline.com. **P.63** *"Pebbles"* martini glass, moserusa.com; *"Atelier"* cocktail shaker by Monique Lhuillier, na.wwrd.com. **P.65** *"Mixology"* glass, na.wwrd.com.

TEQUILA

P.71 *"Mixology" coupes,* na.wwrd.com; *"Arabella" tray,* ralphlaurennhome.com. **P.73** *Nickel julep cups and julep spoon straw,* cocktail kingdom.com. **P.77** *"Bullet" highball glass,* lsa-international.com. **P.81** *"Newport" glass by Theresienthal,* tableartonline.com; *"Loggia" wallpaper,* osborneandlittle.com. **P.83** *"Stroom" glass by Sugahara,* dandelionsf.com; *"Kingsburgh" cocktail shaker,* ralphlaurenhome.com. **P.85** *"Intervalle" highball glass by Saint-Louis,* artedona.com.

RUM

P.87 *"Omega" Champagne glasses by Rogaska,* bestcrystal.com. **P.93** *"Samira" glass by Theresienthal,* tableartonline.com; *swizzle stick by Mystic Prism Studio,* etsy.com. **P.97** *Murano glass bowl from The End of History, 212-647-7598.* **P.99** *"Polka" highball glass,* lsa-international. com. **P.103** *"Fluent" glass,* moserusa.com. **P.105** *"Broughton" glass,* ralphlaurenhome.com.

WHISKEY

P.107 *"Sarjaton" glasses,* iittala.com; *floral bowl,* aerin.com. **P.109** *"Mipreshus" glass,* nouvelstudio.com; *"Crocodilo" wallpaper,* osborneandlittle.com. **P.113** *"Gigolo" glass by Nason Moretti,* tableartonline.com. **P.117** *"Yola" highball glass,* lsa-international.com. **P.121** *"Aspen" glass by Nachtmann,* nachtmannonline.com. **P.123** *"Yukiwa" shaker,* cocktail kingdom.com.

BRANDY

P.127 *"Chandi" glasses by Paola Navone for Egizia,* tableartonline.com. **P.129** *"Excess" pitcher by Saint-Louis,* artedona.com. **P.135** *"Otto" glass by Gottfried Palatin for Theresienthal,* tableartonline.com. **P.139** *"Crosshatch" decanter,* dwellstudio.com. **P.141** *"Savoy" Champagne saucers,* lsa-international.com. **P.143** *"Vita" tall coupe,* williamyeowardcrystal.com.

LIQUEURS & FORTIFIED WINES

P.145 *"Facet" glasses by Lalique,* blooming dales.com; *"Montgomery" cocktail shaker,* ralphlaurenhome.com; *"Fuoco" wallpaper,* trove line.com. **P.147** *"Wiener Stutzen" optic beer glass by Lobmeyr,* tableartonline.com. **P.151** *"Dagny" Champagne glass,* ralphlaurenhome. com. **P.153** *"Ginette" tumbler by Sugahara,* dandelionsf.com. **P.155** *"3/62" Champagne bowl by Nason Moretti,* tableartonline.com. **P.157** *"Herringbone" glass by Artël (in background),* artelglass.com.

MOCKTAILS

P.159 *"Margherita" glasses by Missoni,* replacements.com. **P.161** *"Davina" Champagne saucer,* williamyeowardcrystal.com; *"Primate in Pomp" tray,* michelevarian.com. **P.165** *"Corinne" glass,* williamyeowardcrystal.com. **P.167** *"Night Sky" toasting glasses,* bhldn.com. **P.169** *"Drift Ice" glass,* moserusa.com.

PARTY FOOD

P.171 *Platter by Heath Ceramics,* heath ceramics.com. **P.183** *"Candy Stripe" glass,* lbkstudio.com. **P.195** *Black walnut cutting board,* lostine.com.

MIXOLOGISTS

THESE STAR MIXOLOGISTS CONTRIBUTED THE COCKTAIL AND MOCKTAIL RECIPES IN THIS YEAR'S BOOK.

TONY ABOU-GANIM **P.40** *is a Las Vegas–based spirits expert. He has authored two books,* The Modern Mixologist *and, more recently,* Vodka Distilled.

MAXWELL BRITTEN **P.35** *is the bar director at Maison Premiere, an oyster house and cocktail den in Brooklyn, New York.*

GREG BUTTERA & STEPHEN COLE **P.112** *head the cocktail program at The Barrelhouse Flat in Chicago. Cole, the owner, was previously part of the team at Chicago's The Violet Hour. Buttera, the creative director, came from Aviary/The Office, also in Chicago.*

KATHY CASEY **P.51** *is a chef, mixologist, author and restaurant consultant based in Seattle. Her online cocktail show, Kathy Casey's Liquid Kitchen, can be seen on liquidkitchen.tv.*

ERICK CASTRO **P.56** *is a co-owner and bartender at Polite Provisions in San Diego.*

JULIAN COX **P.76** *co-founded Soigné Group, a beverage consulting firm in L.A. He also spearheaded the cocktail program for Bestia restaurant, among other spots in the L.A. area.*

JOHN DEBARY **P.122** *tends bar at PDT in New York City and is the bar manager for the Momofuku restaurant group. He tested all of the drink recipes for this book.*

JOSH DURR **P.115** *is the founder of Hawthorn Beverage, a beverage consulting firm in Louisville, Kentucky.*

KIRK ESTOPINAL **P.154** *co-owns Cure and Bellocq at The Hotel Modern, both in New Orleans. He is also a co-author of* Beta Cocktails.

CHRIS HANNAH **P.134** *mans the bar at Arnaud's French 75 Bar in New Orleans.*

ERIN HARRIS **P.68** *is the bartender at Jimmy's: An American Restaurant & Bar in Aspen, Colorado.*

MELISSA HAYES **P.149** *manages the bar at Holeman & Finch in Atlanta.*

BOBBY HEUGEL **P.72** *is a co-owner and the cocktail mastermind behind Anvil Bar & Refuge, Underbelly and The Hay Merchant, all in Houston.*

SEAN HOARD **P.29** *manages the bar at Teardrop Cocktail Lounge in Portland, Oregon.*

SEAN KENYON **P.98** *is the owner and bartender at Williams & Graham and manages the bar at The Squeaky Bean, both in Denver. He also writes a cocktail column for the* Denver Westword *newspaper.*

TOMMY KLUS **P.128** *is the curator of the forthcoming Multnomah Whiskey Library in Portland, Oregon, and was the bar program director at Kask, also in Portland.*

IRA KOPLOWITZ & NICHOLAS KOSEVICH **P.32** *founded Bittercube, producers of artisanal bitters in Milwaukee. They are also consulting partners at Eat Street Social in Milwaukee and create cocktail programs for restaurants and bars throughout the Midwest.*

NICOLE LEBEDEVITCH **P.137** *is the bar manager at The Hawthorne in Boston.*

JACK MCGARRY **P.108** *is a co-owner and the head bartender at The Dead Rabbit Grocery and Grog in Manhattan's Financial District.*

PAUL MCGEE **P.92** is a partner at Lettuce Entertain You, a Chicago-based restaurant group. He runs the bar program at Bub City and Three Dots and a Dash, both in Chicago.

IVY MIX **P.48** tends bar at Clover Club in Brooklyn, New York. She also co-founded Speed Rack, a female bartending competition that raises money for breast cancer awareness.

LINDSAY NADER **P.140** is a bartender and writer from Los Angeles whose beverage consulting company is called Elysium Craft Cocktail Services. Most recently a bartender at Pour Vous in L.A., she was also an assistant editor and drinks tester of F&W Cocktails 2011.

BILL NORRIS **P.118** is the beverage director at Midnight Cowboy, Alamo Drafthouse, 400 Rabbits Bar and The Highball, all in Austin, and Glass Half Full in Denver.

GABRIEL ORTA & ELAD ZVI **P.101** are the masterminds behind Bar Lab, a beverage consulting service based in Miami. They are also managing partners at The Broken Shaker, a new outdoor cocktail bar by the pool of the Freehand Miami hostel in Miami Beach.

PATRICIA RICHARDS **P.60** is the master mixologist for Wynn Las Vegas and Encore Resort.

LEO ROBITSCHEK **P.82** manages the bar at Eleven Madison Park and The NoMad Hotel, both in New York City.

JON SANTER **P.95** is the owner and operator of Prizefighter, a bar with a large American whiskey selection in Emeryville, California. He is based in San Francisco.

JOAQUÍN SIMÓ **P.146** & TROY SIDLE **P.148** are partners at Alchemy Consulting, a cocktail bar development company. Their newest project, Pouring Ribbons, opened in New York City in 2012. Simó was also a deputy editor of F&W Cocktails 2009 and 2010.

MATHIAS SIMONIS **P.88** is a member of The Bon Vivants, a San Francisco–based cocktail and spirit consulting company. His latest project is Trick Dog in the Mission District.

JOEL TEITELBAUM **P.44** is the head bartender and bar manager at Harry Denton's Starlight Room in San Francisco.

WILL THOMPSON **P.26** is the head bartender at Drink, a craft-cocktail bar in Boston.

FRANÇOIS VERA **P.80** tends bar at Harvard & Stone in Los Angeles.

JAMES WAMPLER **P.64** is a bartender at The Gin Joint in Charleston, South Carolina.

THANK YOU

In addition to everyone who contributed recipes, the following people were indispensable in making this book possible: Anu Apte, Greg Best, Florent Beuchet, Jacques Bezuidenhout, Greg Boehm, Jamie Boudreau, Derek Brown, Jackson Cannon, Bryan Dayton, Simon Ford, Sean Frederick, John Gertsen, Jason Kosmas, John Lermayer, Katie Loeb, Toby Maloney, Valerie Meehan, Travis Reese, Mike Ryan and Marcos Tello.

FOOD&WINE
BOOKS

More books from
FOOD&WINE

Annual Cookbook
An entire year of FOOD & WINE recipes.

Best of the Best
The best recipes from the 25 best cookbooks of the year.

Wine Guide
Pocket-size guide with the 500 producers you need to know.

TO ORDER, CALL 800-284-4145
OR LOG ON TO **foodandwine.com/books**